photo copiable SWIMMING TECHNIQUE

PE SWIMMING

KS1/2 LESSON PLANS

KELVIN JUBA

First published 2007 by
A & C Black Publishers Ltd
38 Soho Square, London W1D 3HB
www.acblack.com

ISBN-13: 978 0 7136 7786 7

A CIP catalogue record for this book is available from the British Library.

Note: It is always the responsibility of the individual to assess his or her own fitness capability before participating in any training activity. While every effort has been made to ensure the content of this book is as technically accurate as possible, neither the author nor the publishers can accept responsibility for any injury or loss sustained as a result of the use of this material.

Text design by Jocelyn Lucas and Margaret Brain
Cover design by © Paul Oakley, 2007
Cover illustration courtesy of © Paul Oakley, 2007

This book is produced using paper that is made from wood grown in managed, sustainable forests. It is natural, renewable and recyclable. The logging and manufacturing processes conform to the environmental regulations of the country of origin.

Typeset in 10/12.5pt Din-Regular
Printed and bound in the United Kingdom by Caligraving Ltd.

CONTENTS

INTRODUCTION

Swimming is a highly specialised activity yet less than half of all swimming lessons are taken by qualified swimming teachers; the remainder are given by school teachers with some led by adults other than teachers (AOTTs, now known as learning support assistants).

The Ofsted Report of November 2000 'Swimming at Key Stage 2' identified that 83 per cent of pupils could achieve the standard required at Key Stage 2 of swimming 25 metres unaided. At that time, nearly one in five pupils could not achieve the basic standard. Nevertheless, four out of five lessons were described as being good or satisfactory. While partly embracing Key Stage 1, this book is directed towards everyone involved with primary school swimming and water safety, in particular those who work with pupils at Key Stage 2, that is, Years 5 to 6.

Designed as a simple start-to-finish guide, this book aims to give primary school teachers a complete framework for conducting swimming at Key Stage 2. The book explains:

- how to overcome some of the basic day-to-day problems with delivery of lessons, such as transport, budgeting for school swimming and hiring a pool
- which qualifications and courses are available
- how to organise and plan your school swimming for the year
- what equipment is required
- basic swimming teaching techniques, and swimming techniques that should be taught
- how to develop these techniques
- the *DfES Charter for School Swimming*
- how to run top-up swimming
- the records of achievement you would normally be expected to keep
- a scheme of lessons
- a set of resources available to support teachers.

As a whole, this book is designed to build teacher confidence and to encourage school teachers to maximise all swimming resources available to them. The sample lessons found towards the back of the book can be photocopied.

Kelvin Juba
2007

PART 1
GUIDANCE

CHAPTER 1

UNDERSTANDING THE BASIC REQUIREMENTS

Key Stage 1: National Curriculum requirements

Physical Education was recognised as part of the Primary School Curriculum in the Education Act of 1996. Six programmes of study have been drawn up within the National Curriculum for Physical Education and swimming is one of these six programmes. First of all, it is important to understand the requirements at Key Stage 1. These are non-statutory guidelines. Pupils should be taught to:

- move in water (e.g. jump, walk, hop and spin using swimming aids and support)
- float and move, with and without swimming aids
- propel themselves in water using different swimming aids, arm and leg actions and basic strokes.

Key Stage 2: National Curriculum requirements

The Key Stage 2 requirements are that pupils be taught to:

- pace themselves in floating and swimming challenges related to speed, distance and personal survival
- swim unaided for a sustained period over a distance of at least 25 metres
- use recognised arm and leg actions, lying on their front and back
- use a range of recognised strokes and personal survival skills, e.g. front crawl, back crawl, breaststroke, sculling, floating and surface diving.

Additional goals

The difficulty with establishing a standard such as 25 metres is that pupils may think this equates to being safe in water. They need to be made aware that slipping into cold water in rivers, inland waterways and the sea is very different to swimming a short distance in the warm water of a pool.

A distance of 100–200 metres should be the target on front and back, and pupils should be encouraged to breathe underwater at least once in every stroke cycle to aid balance and avoid fatigue.

The ability to climb in and out of the water unaided is another basic skill not directly mentioned at Key Stage 2.

Attainment targets

Pupils are expected to have achieved certain levels of attainment which set out their knowledge and understanding at each Key Stage. These are described in eight levels. Each level comprises a stage and range of performance that pupils should characteristically demonstrate. Pupils at Key Stage 1 are expected to work within levels 1–3 and pupils at Key Stage 2 within levels 2–5. The expected levels of attainment are 2 and 4 respectively.

Table 1 (*see* pages 8–9) is reproduced from the *ASA National Curriculum Resource Pack*. It presents the level descriptions in terms of the aspects of knowledge, skills and understanding specified for the Physical Education programme of study. Some additional text is included to give an indication of how these level descriptions may be applied in the context of swimming.

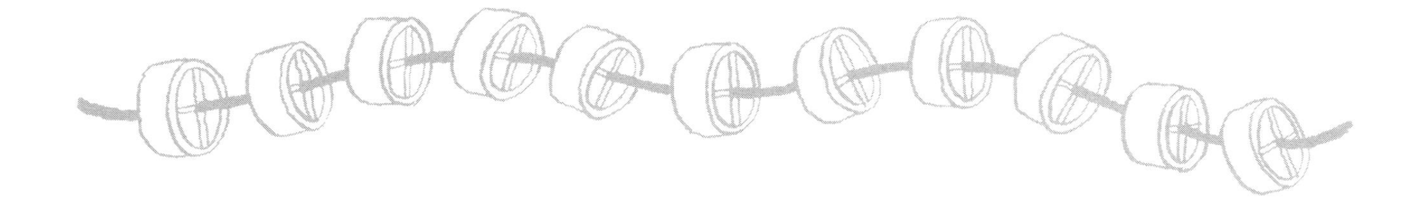

Table 1: National Curriculum attainment targets

Levels	Acquiring and developing skills	Selecting and applying skills, tactics and compositional ideas	Evaluating and improving performance	Knowledge and understanding of fitness and health
1	Pupils copy, repeat and explore simple skills and actions with basic control and co-ordination.	They start to link these skills and actions upright in the water, move and change actions, e.g. walk, hop, jump, skip or turn.	They describe and comment on their own and others' activities. Describe own method used for entering the pool.	They talk about how to exercise safely.
	Safe entries, up to and including swivel entry.	Link these skills and actions in ways that suit the activities.	Describe and comment on their own and others' activities. Share the different ways everybody in the group enters the pool.	Discuss how to move in the water without bumping into each other and how important it is to talk little and quietly.
	Move across a swimming pool to collect an object. Turn and carry the object back to the other side.	Walking upright first, use arms and legs to help move across to the other side of the swimming pool.		Talk about how their body feels during an activity. Describe the way the heart pumps when swimming and compare this with how it pumps when at rest. Describe how the temperature of the water affects their body.
	Use the hands and arms under the water to help movement.			
2	Pupils explore simple skills. They copy, remember, repeat and explore simple actions with control and co-ordination.	They vary skills, actions and ideas, and link these in ways that suit the activities.	They talk about differences between their own and others' performances and suggest improvements.	They understand how to exercise safely.
	Develop submersion skills. Try blowing an *egg flip* across the pool; submerge head and ears; dip into the water to look at own reflection in a mirror; regain standing position from front and back.	Working with a partner, start to link movements, including an entry into the water followed by a method to cross the pool.	Give a commentary on a series of movements, including walking and skipping, used to cross the pool.	Discuss the depth of water and how important it is to stay in own depth while learning to swim.
		Pupils begin to show some understanding of tactics and basic compositional ideas.	Talk about differences between their own and others' performances and suggest improvements.	They describe how their body feels during an activity.
		Add in a rocket-style propulsion to get a good start for the journey across the pool.	Discuss how the movements could be developed by changing speed, height of jumps.	Describe how different activities in the water use different amounts of energy. Compare how the body feels after floating with how it feels after travelling across the pool.
3	Pupils use skills, actions and ideas appropriately.	They select skills, actions and ideas, applying them with co-ordination and control.	They can see how their work is similar to and different from others' work.	They give reasons why warming up before an activity is important.
	Lifting body to a horizontal position, push and glide in streamlined position on front and back, kicking legs and using arms to propel forward.	Use recognised arm and leg actions to move across the pool. Develop efficiency on front and back.	Develop own movements in response to a given series of instructions. Demonstrate ideas to the group. Discuss similarities and differences in interpretation.	Demonstrate an awareness of the need to warm up muscles and get the heart beating faster before swimming.

		Pupils show that they understand tactics and composition by starting to vary how they respond.	They use this understanding to improve their own performance.	They give reasons why physical activity is good for health.
		Begin to develop stamina by using sculling to save energy when on a longer swim.	Refine performance, showing evidence of using suggestions given by the group.	Discuss how swimming supports body weight and, therefore, exercises the body, and that increased swimming activities develop stamina.
4	Pupils link skills, techniques and ideas; their performance shows precision, control and fluency.	Pupils apply skills, techniques and ideas accurately and appropriately.	They compare and comment on skills, techniques and ideas used in their own and others' work.	They explain and apply basic safety principles in preparing for exercise.
	Develop jumping entry. Prepare sequences of movements and moments of stillness in the water, including recognised strokes on front and back, sculling and floating.	Moving across the pool, demonstrate accurate strokes, surface dive for objects and resume swimming to the other side.	When swimming a medley across the pool, watch each others' strokes, including style and breathing techniques. Discuss what makes a good stroke.	Explain how important it is to wear an appropriate costume. Show understanding of the different water depth required for different skills, e.g. jumping.
		Pupils' performance shows that they understand tactics and composition.	They use this understanding to improve performance.	They describe the effects of exercise on their body and how this is valuable to their fitness and health.
		Shown an awareness of others and decide on own strongest stroke when travelling or racing across the pool. Use an entry and propulsion from the side to enhance own performance.	For longer distances, begin to recognise more strokes, comment on speed and how the body feels during the swim. Discuss potential order for medley racing or for developing stamina in the pool.	Describe how swimming causes the body to change and how taking part in exercise promotes an active and healthy lifestyle. Show an understanding that being able to swim is a life skill.
5	Pupils combine their skills, techniques and ideas, consistently showing precision, control and fluency.	Pupils select their skills, techniques and ideas accurately and appropriately. When performing, they draw on what they know about strategy, tactics and composition.	They analyse and comment on how skills, techniques and ideas have been used in their own and others' work.	They explain how the body reacts during different types of exercise, and warm up and cool down in ways that suit the activity.
	Swim across the pool, freeze in a float, surface dive for an object and, finally, swim to the other side. Experiment with different streamlined positions; introduce rotation from vertical and horizontal positions.	Plan with a group how to make the best medley relay team. Show awareness of strengths offered by each member of the team and work on improving group performance.	Be clear about own performance in each stroke. Isolate specific strengths and areas to work on to improve overall performance.	Try different warm-up drills and decide on an order of progression to warm up the body safely. Work similarly for cool down.
			Pupils modify and refine skills and techniques to improve their performance. Begin to record time taken to swim a length and work on improving own performance. Compare with others.	Pupils explain why regular, safe exercise is good for their fitness and health. They demonstrate links between different exercises and how muscle groups can be worked on in different ways.

(Reproduced from the *ASA National Curriculum Resource Pack*, based on a model taken from *Physical Education Assessment, Recording and Reporting at Key Stages 1–4: Guidance for Teachers*, published by the Physical Education Association of the United Kingdom (PEA UK), and the ASA/YST tops cards.)

CHAPTER 2

OVERCOMING THE BARRIERS TO DELIVERY

Initial planning

Start by ensuring that school swimming and water safety forms part of the school's overall action planning, target setting and performance management.

The main factors to consider in planning school swimming lessons are:

- the pool
- the teachers
- the transport
- health and safety.

Hiring the pool

There are a number of different organisations that currently supply school swimming lessons. These include local authorities, trusts, direct services, school sport partnerships, private contractors and pool management companies. Often, however, it is the school's responsibility (and hence the responsibility of the class teacher) to organise the lessons.

When hiring the pool, you will need to consider the following:

- Determine the amount of water-time available for swimming and whether this will fit into your school timetable. A 45-minute swimming lesson at an off-site pool can amount to as much as a double-lesson period when changing and transport is taken into consideration.
- Check the quality of this water-time. For example, how big is the area of a public pool available to your pupils? Is it sufficiently shallow for initial learning? Is it overlooked by an often noisy pool balcony or viewing area?
- Determine the time of day that the water-time is available, particularly if cultural issues are a consideration.
- Consider the cost of the pool. Start early in negotiating a hire rate for the pool. While most pools need to create income, operators recognise that school swimmers are their swimmers of the future. They are, therefore, inclined to look for ways of including your school rather than preventing its participation. You may find it more cost effective to join your resources with one or more other local schools.

Finding the right swimming teacher

In many cases, in a standard class of 30–40 pupils, you will be the second teacher. The swimming teacher needs to hold at least an ASA or STA Teacher Level 2 Certificate. The pool should be able to recommend a suitable swimming teacher but if this information is not available then contact the ASA Customer Services Department (details are listed on page 93) which should be able to advise you on suitable teachers.

More and more pools are providing the cost of a swimming teacher as part of a package with the cost of the pool. On the whole, this tends to reduce the overall cost.

Transport arrangements

It is likely that the most expensive factor will be transport. Fortunately there are a number of ways to reduce transport costs; the most obvious is a number of local schools working together. This works well when transport is booked centrally by the local authority, but almost inevitably becomes more difficult when a handful of schools are involved, as co-ordinating the requirements of each school can be problematic.

Other ways of reducing cost include:

- Smaller classes can be brought by minibus. Many coach companies now have minibuses and most of these companies have spare capacity mid-week. Minibuses can, therefore, be hired at more reasonable rates.
- Community buses are another low-cost alternative which is worth investigating. Although they can only be used for 25 per cent of the day by non-charitable bodies, they may have spare capacity.

Schools that are situated in rural areas find transport barriers more difficult. The swimming lesson inevitably takes up more of the school day and affects the school timetable. One solution may be to have a learning support assistant travel to the pool with the class; another might be to consider the option of taking a double class and use a dry-side facility at a leisure centre in two alternating lessons.

Transport check list

- pupil and all-passenger safety
- weather conditions for travel
- local traffic conditions
- alternative arrangements if the vehicle should break down to cover both transport and finance
- journey time and distance, particularly in relation to the rest of the school timetable for the day
- the level of insurance cover
- appropriate levels of supervision
- competence and training of the driver – it needs to be determined whether the driver has the appropriate training and a valid licence for the vehicle to be utilised for the journey.

Safe practice with transport to pools

In the past, pupil behaviour has been a major contributor to accidents on school journeys, so discipline is an important consideration throughout the whole swimming session. The driver is not responsible for pupil supervision and the school should ensure that a risk assessment prior to the journey has established an appropriate and adequate level of supervision. This includes the safety of the pupils away from the bus in crossing roads, for example. During the journey, the group leader should make pupils aware of where the emergency door is situated and the location of the first-aid kit and anti-fire equipment.

All teachers (as well as the governing body of the school) should ensure that all travel arrangements are suitable for the visit. All minibuses and coaches, which carry groups of three or more children aged between 3 and 15 years inclusive, must be fitted with a seat belt for each pupil. The seats have to face forward and seat restraints should comply with the legal requirements.

While operators of coaches and buses are legally required to be licensed, it is always best to hire transport from a reputable company and to ensure that operators have the appropriate public service vehicle (PSV) licence.

If a school minibus is to be used, adults over 21 years of age who have a normal driving licence (categories A, B and C) can drive pupils by minibus providing:

- it is part of their employment
- they have a clean driving licence
- their employment contract states that they can be responsible for transport.

It is probably wise not to use a member of staff who has a poor driving record as the driver is responsible for the vehicle during the visit.

The capacity for the minibus should be 16 pupils plus the teacher/driver and, again, a forward-facing seat with seat belt should be provided for each pupil. The minibus should also comply with the regulations on fittings and basic construction. The minibus's condition should be checked on a weekly basis, it should be regularly serviced by a reputable garage, and a record-of-use book maintained.

While the chair of the school governors or the head teacher is ultimately responsible for the minibus, all those in the school who drive it should receive driving instruction and training on the management of passengers. The best sources of information and advice can be found on the Royal Society for Prevention of Accidents web site (www.rospa.com), and by obtaining the Minibus Conditions of Fitness, Equipment and Use Regulations 1977 as well as the Road Vehicle Construction and Use Regulations 1996.

Remember that disabled passengers may need provision that is specific to their needs. Wheelchair users, for example, should have access via a ramp and a means of securing the chair; these will need to be checked prior to hire.

The cost of transport is a big barrier to school swimming. Many schools are now charging parents or are being funded by PTAs. Other schools are turning to parents and teachers to provide transport in private cars. This practice brings other safety considerations.

- First, teachers should ensure that the car is roadworthy and that the volunteer is vetted.
- Second, teachers should satisfy themselves that the driver holds an appropriate licence and insurance cover to drive pupils to the pool, and that the driver is aware of his or her legal responsibilities in driving pupils.
- Third, a parental consent form must be signed by each parent giving permission for their child to be transported by another person.
- Finally, drivers should not be put in a position where they are alone with a pupil.

Much of this process will already be common practice in schools and, by following a few straightforward practices, future difficulties can be avoided.

Making the journey an opportunity

Long journeys can be used for water safety education, cross-curricular tasks and as an opportunity to encourage pupils to relate their experiences at the pool to the rest of the class and to highlight achievement on the part of individual pupils.

Swimming can link with English, Mathematics, Science, Design and Technology, and Geography. Pupils could be asked:

- How far did you manage to swim today?
- Estimate how far it is from one side of the pool to the other.
- How long is the big pool at the facility?
- How far along the big pool would your furthest swim today take you?
- How much further do you need to swim to complete the distance needed for the Key Stage 2 standard?
- How many widths of the learner's pool would you need to swim to complete 25 metres? 100 metres?
- How many metres did everyone in the group swim today without stopping?
- What is the total distance swum by the group today when making their furthest swim?

You might also connect the swimming occasion to the 2012 London Olympics. Questions could include:

- How long will the pool be at the London Olympics?
- How many lengths would you have to swim of the Olympic pool if you were taking part in the 400 metres?
- Which is the longest Olympic swimming event?
- How many pool lengths are there in the 1500 metres?

Co-ordinating school swimming

In summary, Figure 1 is a schematic diagram showing the sequence necessary to organise swimming for your school class.

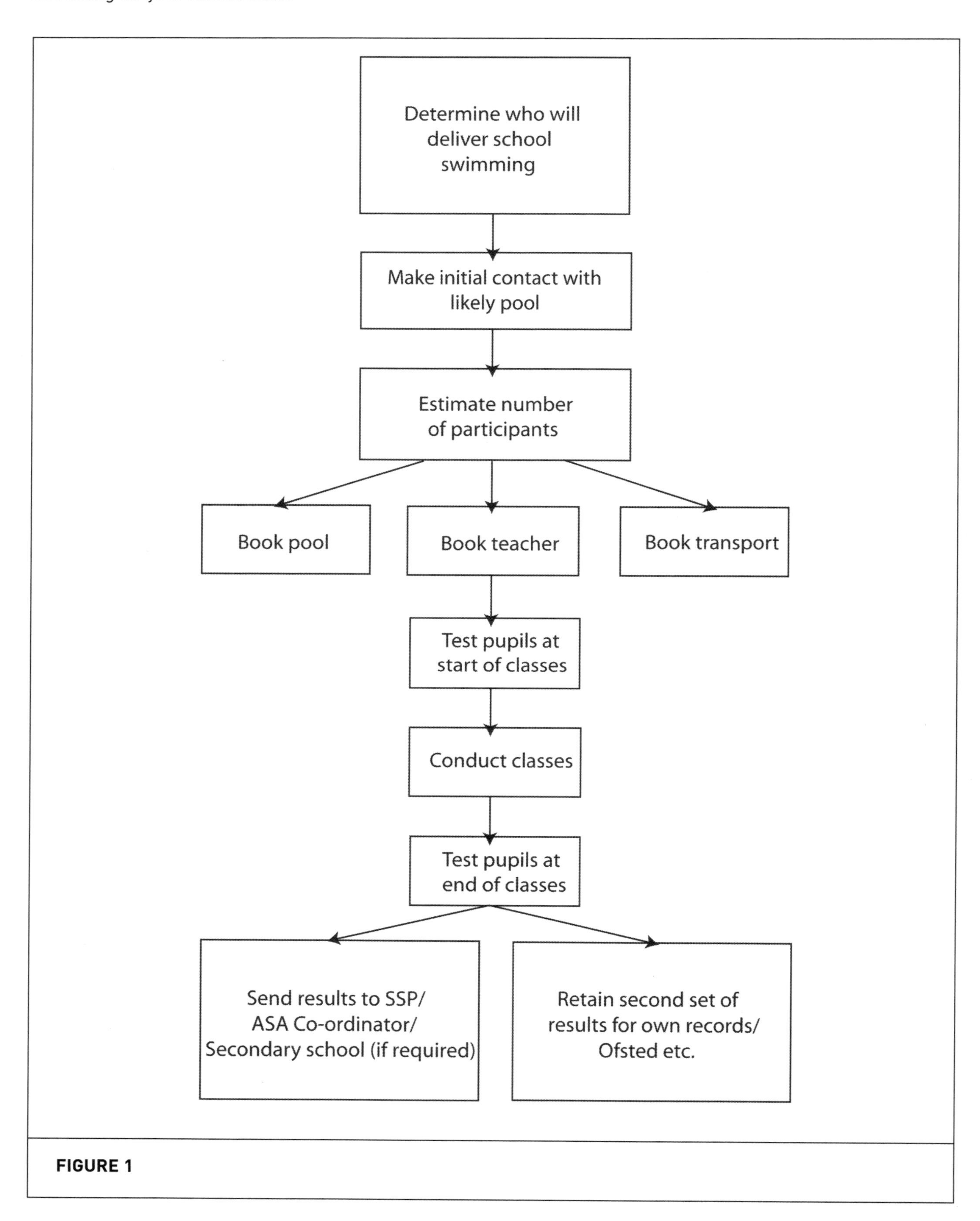

FIGURE 1

Family cultures

Like much of the learning process, a supportive home culture is very important. If a child is not encouraged to swim at home or swimming is not emphasised, he or she will find learning to swim via school lessons more difficult. Often swimming is not considered important within many families; they do not swim as a family unit and so do not have a shared experience of the enjoyment of swimming. School swimming lessons should be regular and conducted over a period of months, even years, in order that vital steps in the learning process are not missed.

ASA and DfES top-up lessons pilot scheme

In 2003, the Amateur Swimming Association (ASA) and the Department for Education and Skills (DfES) commissioned a pilot scheme of swimming top-up lessons in Bristol and Durham for those pupils who had been unable to achieve the Key Stage 2 Standard in swimming (*see* Chapter 7). It was found that being part of an ethnic minority was not a barrier to being able to swim. During the top-up lessons, minority groups learnt just as quickly as white British groups. Being part of an ethnic minority and struggling with cultural resistance to swimming was, however, a major barrier.

Children from economically and socially deprived backgrounds are often considered at a disadvantage when it comes to swimming. During the top-up pilot scheme, it was found that, given the right circumstances, a pupil from a disadvantaged background was just as likely to be able to learn to swim as a more advantaged pupil. These circumstances were:

- if a pool was within walking or low-cost travel distance
- if an older sibling swam
- if the pool entry cost was reasonably affordable (as was found in many cases)
- if the child was encouraged to go swimming by his or her parents.

Objections by religious groups to body exposure can be overcome by sewing together long-sleeved lightweight t-shirts and trousers (even wearing pyjama trousers). This solution was being provided on a home-made basis by the parents of one school participating in the pilot scheme.

School swimming culture

Good school swimming cultures manifest themselves in a number of ways: regular and consistent programmes of lessons, attention to water safety education in the classroom, reference to the importance of swimming, strong participation by teachers during lessons at the pool side, and verbal reference to certificates, badges and achievements during assemblies and presentation days. To encourage this, explain the importance of swimming practice to pupils (and, where possible, to parents) at local pools in non-school hours.

Often those pupils who are experiencing difficulties in general, either through low self-esteem, obesity, learning difficulties or shyness, are those 'most at risk' of not learning. Early identification of such pupils can be of benefit, since they can be placed in a learning group with a much lower teacher–pupil ratio or in a group where they are with others who have the same difficulties. A large learn-to-swim class often exacerbates these difficulties.

On the journey back from the pool, create a small swimming community by giving pupils the opportunity to recount their experiences to others. If this is not possible, then a one- or two-minute reference to pupils' achievements can be made within the classroom. Self-esteem and enthusiasm can be encouraged by positively reinforcing achievements on returning to school and heralding success among the generally unsuccessful pupils.

Charting pupils' achievements is also important and these records are often overlooked. Examples of charts can be found in Chapter 8 (*see* pages 39–43).

It is not uncommon for pupils to arrive at school or at the pool without a swimming costume. The reason for this is generally economic or social. The best schools always have spare ready-washed swimming costumes for those who cannot swim because their families cannot afford, or do not provide, swim wear. Goggles are discouraged in many school swimming lessons, but where they are allowed, ensure that spare pairs are available. Second-hand costumes and goggles will often be a solution.

Education in the classroom

In addition to the cross-curricular links outlined in 'Making the journey an opportunity' (*see* page 13), dry-side education should include basic hygiene, water safety and good practice at swimming pools. These are all explained in detail in the *ASA National Curriculum Resource Pack for Swimming and Water Safety* (details of how to contact the ASA are found on page 93).

Hygiene at the pool

Make pupils aware that, just as they expect to find a clean pool, they need to adopt hygienic habits to make the environment better for others. For those individuals who will never experience going to the pool with their parents or family, the class teacher has an important role in encouraging high standards. The classroom is the best place to reinforce some of the key principles.

Some of the basic instructions to pupils should be:

- Wear a swimming cap, particularly if you have long hair, or tie long hair back.
- Do not wear jewellery and watches while attending the pool.
- Shower well before entering, and after leaving, the pool.
- Use the toilet prior to entering the pool – preferably not during the pool session.
- Dry thoroughly and make sure that you dry between the toes.
- If there is sufficient time, use the hairdryer, especially on cold days.
- Make sure that your hair is dry before leaving the building.
- Depending on weather conditions, wear sufficiently warm clothing after leaving the pool building; this includes covering the head.
- Clean the soles and tops of your shoes before entering the changing area.
- Inform the teacher if you feel unwell before going to the pool or if there is any other cause for concern.

You should exclude a pupil from swimming lessons until he or she has recovered from any of the following conditions:

- a stomach illness that has caused diarrhoea
- infectious diseases
- open wounds
- coughs, colds and related infections such as catarrh, sinusitis
- sore eyes
- ear infections.

Sometimes it is difficult to know whether to exclude a pupil because of a medical condition so, if in doubt, ask the pupil to return when they have consulted a family doctor for his or her opinion.

The Institute of Sport and Recreation Management (ISRM) will be able to advise on the most up-to-date standards within pools (contact details are given on page 94).

Linking swimming to the health agenda

There are a number of opportunities to explain the health benefits of swimming. This means:

- explaining the importance of regular exercise, including swimming
- outlining the importance of the physical and mental approaches towards life
- encouraging pupils to eat healthy options while at the pool, i.e. drinking bottled water afterwards rather than fizzy drinks; avoiding unhealthy options sometimes offered through vending machines
- explaining that pupils should avoid swimming within an hour of eating a meal.

Good practice at swimming pools

Many swimming pools display notices about acceptable behaviour. The teacher should highlight this information to pupils in a classroom situation prior to the first lesson.

Some general examples of good practice by schools include the following:

- Encourage a high level of discipline because learner swimmers are in a situation where they could be in danger.
- Ensure that when a whistle is blown or a teacher calls to the whole class, pupils stabilise their body position immediately, either by standing on the bottom or holding on to or standing at the pool side.
- Avoid blocking entrances and doors while queuing at the pool.
- Show consideration by waiting for adults to enter and exit through a door, particularly parents with young children and babies.
- Other pool users are at risk from pupils' actions so pupils should not intrude on other people's space in the water or impair their ability to carry out their chosen activity.
- Avoid splashing and high noise levels.

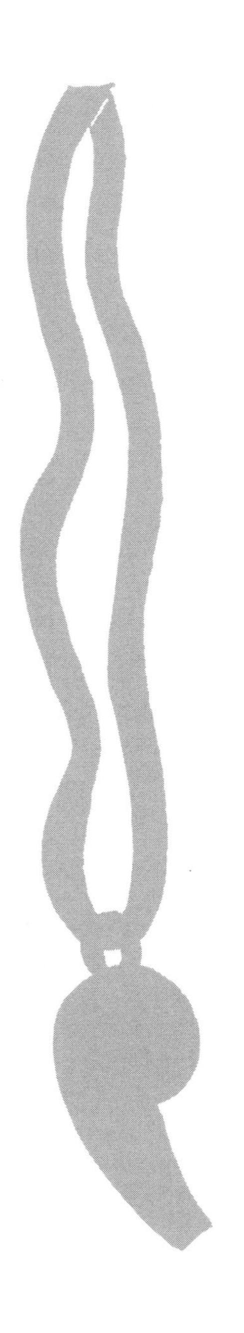

Safety issues for the class teacher at the pool

While the driver may be responsible for the journey by coach, the class teacher or his/her designated representatives are acting *in loco parentis*. This responsibility commences from the point of leaving the classroom until pupils return to the school. In the pool, even if the lesson is being conducted by a swimming teacher or other person the duty of care rests solely with the school teacher. New practices are currently being introduced which mean that local agreements may vary this practice.

The school teacher must consider the following points:

- Is there a well-documented emergency action procedure for the pool being used?
- Can pupils be easily identified by the school (or pool) staff?
- What is the emergency signal and do pupils understand this signal?
- What action should pupils take following the emergency signal (e.g. stop, look, listen, clear the pool)? At which point should pupils leave the pool?
- What actions should you and other school staff take in an emergency situation?
- What actions will pool staff take in an emergency situation?
- Where are life-saving aids positioned? Are you familiar with these?
- How would you contact the emergency services? (Check to see if the pool has a phone and always carry a working mobile phone.)

- Is the emergency action procedure based on differing numbers of pool staff at the pool side, particularly if there is only one member of pool side staff?
- What emergency procedure needs to be modified if the school does not have exclusive use of the pool?
- What aftercare may be needed, and how and by whom would this be provided?
- Is there an existing reporting procedure for accidents and, if so, what is this reporting procedure?
- Write down, or obtain, a copy of the swimming pool accident procedure. Ensure that all members of school/designated staff, including yourself, receive a copy. This procedure should be practised on a regular basis and the dates of those practices recorded.
- Is adequate changing supervision provided?
- Do not allow children in the pool if the bottom of the pool is not clearly visible.

Further details on safety issues can be found through the *ASA National Curriculum Resource Pack* or by reading the ASA/DfES's *National Top Up Swimming Scheme Toolkit*. These can be found on each organisation's web site (*see* details on page 96). The Resource Pack also carries useful general principles and considerations before going to the pool.

Water safety

Although water safety should be taught in the classroom, preferably by an expert brought in to the school, the coach journey to a swimming pool is a good opportunity to reinforce some of the more important aspects. Water safety education should emphasise drowning prevention, and lessons should highlight the key points of the Water Safety Code. The code, which has been developed by Lifesavers and the Royal Society for the Prevention of Accidents (RoSPA), is also endorsed by the ASA. It states:

- spot the dangers
- take safety advice
- go with a friend
- learn how to help.

Pupils should be taught the Water Safety Code from Year 1 and tested orally on their knowledge during Key Stages 1 and 2.

You may decide that each of the four points of the Water Safety Code will be presented to pupils over four lessons. A series of factors that are linked in a sequence contribute to what is commonly known as the 'Drowning Chain' and it is worth making your pupils aware of these. The chain is as follows:

- lack of water safety education, lack of attention or misjudgement of one's own ability
- uninformed or unprotected access to the hazard area, including lack of safety advice
- incompetent supervision or lack of any supervision, especially of the young and older people
- the inability to cope once an emergency has arisen.

Planning water safety lessons

A typical water safety lesson based on 'spot the dangers' might be as follows:

"Many people go on holiday to the seaside. All open water can have dangers. You should be able to spot the signs and take action to avoid that danger. Let's imagine you are going to the beach for the very first time...

- Tell me about some of the dangers at the beach you already know about.
- How will you know if it is dangerous to enter the water?
- What do the warning flags look like?"

Perhaps use a photograph of a seaside scene, for example:

"Now look at this photograph of people at the seaside.

- Can you see any warning flags?
- If so, where are they situated?
- Are there lifeguards and a lifeguard station present?
- Tell me about those people over there: would you say they are entering the sea at a safe point?
- Other than swimming, what other things are people doing in the water?
- If you were entering the water at this beach, can you see any places where you think it would be safe enough to swim?
- Can you see places where you think it might be dangerous? Why?
- What about these people over here who are in a boat? And those over there who are surfing? Can you see anything else – yes, there is one person on a jet ski.
- What other things would you have to think about if you were going in the water?
- What about water temperature (e.g. the dangers of cold water)?
- Would you have a friend with you?
- Do you have a meeting point if one of you gets lost?
- Which direction would you swim in?"

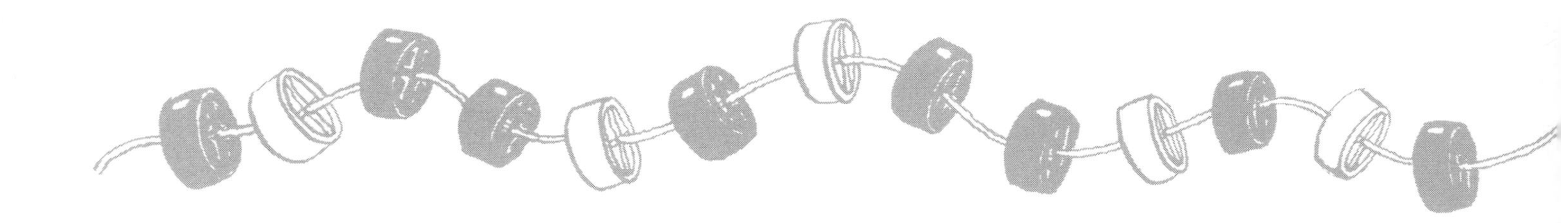

The lesson could continue further, for example:

"We've looked at the photograph but there are one or two other things that we should be thinking about:

- Look at the beach and consider whether it is too stony or whether it has debris that might damage your feet.
- What about closeness to the rocks when you enter the water?
- Now think about rock pools.
- Can you see the lifeguard from where you are swimming?
- Check on the tides – when is it high tide and how quickly does the tide come in?
- Which way is the tide flowing?
- Do you know how deep the water is before entering?
- Are there plenty of other bathers around you?
- I want you to draw me a picture or a small plan of the beach. Show me the position of the flags, lifeguards, first aid point and any hazards, and then show me where you would enter the water."

CHAPTER 3

HOW TO BECOME QUALIFIED AND LEARN MORE

The swimming education landscape is changing rapidly, so it is important to keep up to date with the latest developments. Many classroom teachers may not have renewed their swimming qualification for a number of years and it is recommended that you visit the Amateur Swimming Association web site (www.britishswimming.org) in order to see what is currently available. Some teaching and coaching qualifications in Wales and Scotland might be slightly different to those in England; Scottish teachers might like to visit the Scottish Swimming web site (www.scottishswimming.com) or contact Scottish Swimming, National Swimming Academy, University of Stirling, Stirling, FK9 4LA; Welsh teachers can access the web site of the Welsh Amateur Swimming Association (www.welshasa.co.uk) or contact Swim Wales Education and Training, Wales National Pool Swansea, Sketty Lane, Swansea, SA2 8QG.

The Amateur Swimming Association (ASA), which is the national governing body for swimming in England, is currently reviewing its teaching qualifications so that they are aligned to the UK Coaching Certificate Awards. These awards are designed to bring commonality to standards across sport and to allow transference, where appropriate, of knowledge from sport to sport. They embrace teaching, sports development and coaching.

ASA swimming qualifications

The current framework for swimming qualifications offered by the ASA involves four levels of swimming teacher, with a further specific qualification for school teachers. The qualifications are described below.

Helper Certificate

This introductory, entry-level qualification is useful if you plan to assist in regular swimming lessons. It is designed for those who want to help with class and group activities under the guidance of someone holding ASA Level 2 Certificate for Teaching Swimming (see below). You must be older than 14 years of age to take the course which lasts for eight hours.

Level 1 Certificate for Teaching Swimming

This is the first main qualification in teaching and coaching. It is designed for those assisting teachers, working under supervision while teaching a limited range of basic skills to a group of up to four participants. This can be increased to six participants if the teacher has sufficient experience and if a risk assessment has been carried out by the supervising teacher. Candidates must be a minimum of 16 years of age at the start of the course, which lasts for approximately 27.5 hours.

Level 2 Certificate for Teaching Swimming

This is the main teaching certificate and used to be called the ASA Teachers Certificate. It qualifies you to teach swimming unsupervised to classes of up to 12 participants, from non-swimmers to any gifted pupils who might want to be involved in pre-competition development. To pursue this qualification you need to be 18 years of age and hold the ASA Level 1 Certificate or the ASA Primary School Teachers Certificate for the teaching of swimming, and have completed 15 hours verified teaching since achieving the Level 1 Certificate.

Holding the Level 2 Certificate allows you to organise and supervise Level 1 teachers and other helpers. The certificate is graded according to whether you complete a three-unit course lasting 41.25 hours, or a four-unit course lasting 59.75 hours. Assessment is carried out through a log book, written examinations and practical teaching.

Level 3 Certificate for the Development and Management of Swimming Programmes

This is a more advanced certificate for those wishing to assist organisations such as local education authorities, swimming clubs and local authority sport and leisure development departments in providing swimming programmes. It comprises four units: planning the swimming programme; developing and improving the programme; managing and developing oneself and other members of staff; developing enhanced teaching skills for swimming. The pre-requisites are an ASA Level 2 Certificate for Teaching Swimming plus an ASA Level 2 in a second discipline. There are 300 learning hours in total, broken down into 40, 40, 60 and 70 hours for the four units respectively, 20 hours of portfolio preparation and 10 hours of assessment visits, as well as 60 hours of additional ASA qualifications.

Swimming qualifications for school teachers

There are a number of courses specifically for school teachers.

The National Curriculum Training Programme

Through Module 1 a qualified teacher is equipped to coach a limited range of basic aquatic techniques to small groups. The course embraces basic technical knowledge, health and safety, the transference of existing skills into the pool environment, and familiarisation with Top Sport Swimming and the National Plan for Teaching Swimming. The course amounts to three hours theoretical work, two hours Top Sport Swimming and two hours practical work.

Module 2 requires the candidate to already hold Module 1 and be a qualified school teacher. Each of the subjects in Module 1 is covered in more depth. Module 2 consists of six hours theoretical and four hours practical work.

The Primary School Teacher Certificate for the Teaching of Swimming builds on Modules 1 and 2 and comprises nine hours theoretical content, two hours of Top Sport Swimming and six hours practical work.

Introduction to Top Sport Swimming

This course can also be invaluable to teachers. It enables a school teacher to introduce Top Sport Swimming into a schools swimming programme. This is a non-assessed course lasting for three hours.

Other qualifications

ASA/Sportscoach UK Good Practice and Child Protection

This is a course rather than a certificate but can be used as evidence of having attended an accredited child protection seminar in swimming. The workshop aims to identify good coaching practice to promote positive relations with children. It presents ways of dealing with your own feelings about child abuse and highlights situations where coaching might be considered to be poor practice or even child abuse. It outlines the symptoms of abuse and identifies appropriate action to deal with this. The seminar explains how to act if a child reveals that he or she has been abused and describes the appropriate practice that reduces the likelihood of abuse occurring. The seminar lasts for three hours.

CPD online

The ASA is currently in the process of creating online learning modules for teachers. The first of these, 'The principles of good freestyle', can be found by visiting the web site of the Centre for Aquatics Research and Education (CARE) at the University of Edinburgh (www.care.ed.ac.uk). A full scheme of online modules has also been developed by Swim Trainers and these can be found at the swim-IQ web site (www.swimtrainers.com).

The Helper Certificate

The pre-requisite for this course is that the adult should be associated with a school, for example as a school ancillary, nursery nurse, learning support staff member or a parent, guardian, carer or grandparent.

Learning support assistants are being called on more and more to assist with school swimming. This qualification provides people who would like to help the class swimming teacher with knowledge of the requirements for swimming at Key Stage 1 and/or 2. It also covers a basic knowledge of the four strokes, safety at the pool, and skills required to assist the Designated Swimming Teacher (DST) in the delivery of the swimming lesson. The course consists of five hours theoretical work and two hours practical work.

National Vocational Qualifications (NVQs) and Scottish Vocational Qualifications (SVQs)

NVQs and SVQs are available in Sport, Recreation and Allied Occupations. NVQs test the candidate's competence in the workplace. There is a generic Level 1 award in Active Leisure and Learning, which provides a pathway into NVQs/SVQs at Level 2. NVQ/SVQ Levels 2 and 3 in Coaching, Teaching and Instructing (which were revised in 2002) are awarded in the context of a specific sport/activity and age group. The ASA Level 2 Certificate can be used as Accreditation of Prior Achievement (APA). The assessments for NVQ Level 2 are made against the performance criteria of the National Occupational Standards in Sport and Recreation and Allied Occupations (teaching/coaching and instructing) in the context of swimming and its associated disciplines.

Swimming Teachers Association (STA) qualifications

The Swimming Teachers Association (STA) runs a series of courses for swimming teachers and teachers in schools. It also organises classes for aquatic aerobics teaching (aquacise). The qualifications offered in this area are:

- **STA Level 2 Swimming Teachers Certificate, Beginners.**
  Candidates need to be at least 16 years of age, hold a life-saving qualification approved by the STA and be able to swim at least 25 metres. The Level 2 Certificate enables you to teach classes of up to 10 beginners unsupervised, and larger groups, if supervised.

- **STA Level 2 Swimming Teachers Certificate, Full.**
  Candidates have to be at least 18 years of age, hold an approved life-saving qualification, have achieved the STA Level 2 Swimming Teachers Certificate or equivalent qualification, and preferably have had some post-qualification experience of teaching swimming. The qualification enables individuals to teach classes of all sizes and levels of ability, without supervision.

To achieve either qualification, students are assessed during the course and complete final practical and written examinations.

A further award offered by the STA may also impact on those wishing to qualify as swimming teaching helpers and assistants. The Student Teacher Certificate for 13 to 18-year-olds is a first step to a career as a swimming teacher. Candidates must hold a life-saving certificate approved by the STA and have worked under the guidance of a qualified teacher for at least five hours.

Royal Life Saving Society qualifications

Lifesavers, or the Royal Life Saving Society, offers qualifications for teachers who wish to become more proficient in life saving.

- The bronze medallion is recognised as the standard award for life saving, developing fitness, knowledge, skill and judgement. All those who wish to deliver school swimming should hold this qualification.
- The next stage is the Award of Merit where Life Support 2 is achieved.
- The third stage is the Distinction, which requires Life Support 3 and the Silver Cross Open Award.

There are two further awards – the Bronze and Silver Cross – but these mainly apply to the ability to perform open water rescue.

The Life Support Awards train the individual in emergency procedures, including casualty assessment and the stages of resuscitation. There are three levels of award with the more advanced stage being the National Lifeguard Qualification. The seventh edition of the award was introduced in January 2004.

Learning support assistants may find the Community Life Support award, a two-hour course for members of the community, a useful entry point to life saving. Details of all courses can be obtained on the Lifesavers web site (www.lifesavers.org.uk).

CHAPTER 4

HOW TO ORGANISE SCHOOL SWIMMING

When planning the school year the overall aim should be to teach front crawl, backstroke and breaststroke to a preliminary level, and a range of water skills to the more advanced swimmers.

Although it would be highly desirable to run swimming once a week or more for 40 weeks a year, the reality is that pressures of SATS and academic elements of the National Curriculum mean that many schools, unless they have their own pool, deliver between 12 and 30 weeks swimming a year.

Many schools with two classes in Year 6 will deliver, approximately, a 15-week block of lessons to each class. Given these constraints, you probably should be planning the practical side of your swimming programme along very broad lines. For instance, your sessions might look like this:

- Lesson 1 – acquaintance with the water.
- Lessons 2 and 3 – water confidence, water games and some basic water skills.
- Lesson 4 – introduction of crawl leg kick, breathing and dog paddle.
- Lesson 5 – more dog paddle, getting in and out of the water and further water skills.
- Lesson 6 – introduction of kicking on the back, jumping into the water and front crawl breathing and arms.
- Lesson 7 – front crawl, treading water, sitting dive.
- Lesson 8 – front crawl, backstroke legs, more advanced water skills.
- Lesson 9 – front crawl, introduction of backstroke arms and breathing.
- Lesson 10 – front crawl, backstroke, further work on introduction to diving.
- Lesson 11 – introduction of breaststroke, diving from pool side, surface diving.
- Lessons 12 to 14 – general all-round work on the three strokes already learnt.
- Lesson 15 – testing and recording for the National Curriculum.

Which pupils go and when

The age at which pupils should start their school swimming varies from one school to another. Many now provide school swimming in Year 5 as this frees up Year 6 to concentrate on SATS and also makes it easier to identify those pupils who will require top-up lessons, probably in Year 6.

Top-up lessons are now being offered on a national basis for those pupils unable to achieve the Key Stage 2 standard towards the end of their final year at primary school. You will need to start to identify possible candidates from as early as February to ensure they are fully catered for in the summer term. (For more on top-up swimming, *see* Chapter 7.)

Your class will probably need to be divided into two or three groups; those pupils with some swimming experience forming a more advanced group down to those pupils that have genuine fears. In booking a public pool, try to find a time when the group with no experience can be introduced to a learner's pool that has no other groups occupying it. A pool without distraction which is not overlooked is also advantageous. If you are fortunate enough to have a learner's pool with a graduated entrance, this is a further advantage.

Breaking down the teaching roles

You will need to decide what roles the adults will fulfil while pupils are at the pool. Generally, a qualified swimming teacher will take responsibility for the weaker swimmers. However, where the class teacher has a more advanced qualification in swimming teaching, it is a good idea to reverse the roles as the class teacher will have the added advantage of knowing each pupil individually.

It is advisable to use adult support assistants where you feel they can add to the learning process. This generally means using them in a support role within each group rather than the lead role, although there will be exceptions to this: where a learning support assistant is appropriately qualified, he or she will be able to lead a group. Common sense has to be applied in these situations. In general, the target class ratios should be one teacher to 12 pupils and, where this is not possible, the ratio of one teacher to 15 pupils should be the absolute maximum.

Structuring the lesson

The general structure of the lesson should consist of the following:

- set up
- main theme
- contrasting activity
- keeping records.

Set up

Before the lessons starts, make certain that:

- the part of the pool where you expect to take the lesson is available
- you know the dimensions and depth of the pool
- you understand the written emergency operating procedures
- you have suitable pool side shoes and clothing which will allow ease of pool side demonstration
- you determine the various points on the pool side where you will conduct the lesson and make sure you can be clearly seen at these points
- you carry a whistle or have an alternative strategy for drawing the attention of the whole class.

Orientation

- ❍ Make sure that all pupils are on the pool side before you begin.
- ❍ Make sure all class members know which group they are in.
- ❍ Set down rules for the class.
- ❍ Ensure pupils know which point they should be starting from and that they understand safe points of entry and exit, and actions to take in the case of an accident or injury.
- ❍ Brief pupils so that they know when to stop, look and listen.
- ❍ Check on attire to be certain that no pupil is wearing something unsuitable and that all apparel is secure.
- ❍ Introduce what you expect to cover in the lesson.

Main theme

- ❍ Aim to focus the learning on developing one key element or stroke.
- ❍ Demonstrate both on the pool side and through a pupil who can already carry out the skill.
- ❍ Make the skill progressive through introducing a number of stages which can be worked on individually, and then allow for the whole skill to be developed.
- ❍ Allow for feedback from pupils.

Contrasting activity

- ❍ This may take the form of a whole group activity, such as games or a water skill.
- ❍ It should aim to provide a completely different type of challenge to pupils.
- ❍ After the initial stages of learning, pupils can be encouraged to measure what they are achieving in later lessons.

Keeping records

- ❍ Always keep a record of each lesson.
- ❍ Make a note of how the lesson went as a whole in relation to the overall programme you set yourself at the start of the year.
- ❍ Keep a record of those pupils that may need extra help over the next few lessons as well as the particular skills in which they require assistance.
- ❍ Earmark those pupils that may need top-up lessons in the future.
- ❍ Towards the end of the overall programme, you will need to keep records for Key Stage 2 assessment.

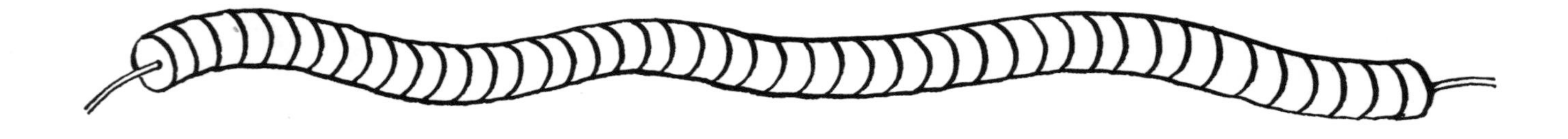

Accommodating obese pupils

Problems with obesity are exacerbated in school swimming situations. This is not only because it is the one activity where pupils are required to reveal much of their body, but also because the first stages of entering the water can be stressful and these feelings of stress can be further heightened with body image issues.

Two useful ways of working with obesity are:

- First, allow those pupils who are conscious of their body to enter the water before other pupils have arrived on the pool side.
- Second, allow them to wear t-shirts to cover their upper body. Some would argue that this is a bad idea and will create extra drag in the water. If, however, this is the only way to get a pupil even to contemplate entering the water, then it should be considered, particularly for activities which require the pupil to stand in shallow water.

Talented swimmers

Almost inevitably you will be faced with a wide range of abilities in your class. Some pupils will have had the chance to swim before, others will have never been into a pool. Catering for this range is a challenge and it can become even more so if you are also faced with the prospect of a very talented young swimmer. The question of what to do with him/her is for the future as much as for your current lesson.

The solution is to find out more about the comprehensive national framework the ASA has established for Long Term Athlete Development (LTAD). This framework has been established for teachers and coaches in order to identify and nurture the more obviously gifted pupils.

If you are fortunate enough to have a gifted pupil, you may want to visit the ASA web site (www.britishswimming.org), where you will find a link to *A Shorter Guide to Long Term Athlete Development (LTAD)*. This useful four-page guide sets out swimming for the talented in five stages. The first two stages refer to primary school swimming. Stage 1 considers swimming for pupils aged 5–8 years (female) and 6–9 years (male). This stage is entitled *FUNdamental* and is based on swimming being structured and fun. Stage 2, which is for pupils aged 8–11 years (female) and 9–12 years (male), is entitled *Swim Skills: Building Technique*. It is worth a visit to this web site to learn more about the issues for the talented. All too often consideration is given to weaker swimmers in an effort to help to get them started, while the very talented are not sufficiently catered for.

Disability pupils

While disabled pupils will often have their own lessons independent of the able bodied, there will occasionally be pupils with a slight disability who are included in a general class situation. These pupils need to be treated with appropriate sensibilities. Most disabled people would both want to and are capable of taking part in 'open' unstructured sessions. In the early stages, you may need to think about getting assistance from within the school for those disabled swimmers who need to undergo confidence-building activities. You may also need to think about bringing these pupils to the pool separately, by choosing a time when the pool is quieter, in order to carry out these activities.

If you are organising a swimming lesson for a group of disabled pupils, you will need to bear one or two overarching points in mind. First, determine the size of the class. As a guide, 20 pupils is a good maximum working number as the class teacher and pool operator will also need to ensure there is sufficient space for carers to help with lifting and holding some participants. The number of carers and supporters will also need to be determined in advance as the level of assistance will vary from individual to individual. As the class teacher, you are likely to have your own carers but, in some cases, you may want to plan ahead with your pool operator, who may be able to help with suitable carers by approaching disabled groups/clubs that already use the pool. The overall session should also be led by an appropriately qualified swimming teacher, i.e. a teacher with the ASA Level 1 or 2 Teachers for Swimmers with a Disability certificate.

A further point that will need consideration is at what time of day to hold the session. This will be based on a number of factors – the availability of assistants and a lead teacher, the ease of use of changing facilities, and the availability of suitable transport, such as community transport, during the selected period of the day. If it is too late in the afternoon, it may be difficult to provide suitable transport.

Any carers should be trained in Disability Equality issues and, if possible, have been on a Sportscoach UK course such as Working with Disabled Sportspeople. Class teachers should also ensure that a facilities audit has been carried out which ensures that the facility being used comes under the Disability and Discrimination Act, Part 3.

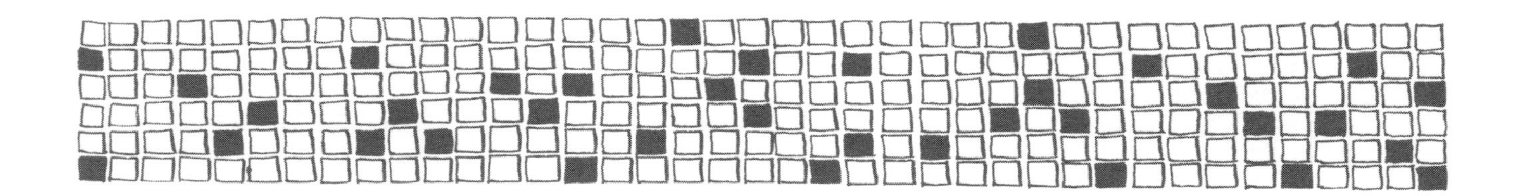

CHAPTER 5

PLANNING YOUR SWIMMING YEAR

National Plan for Teaching Swimming

The ASA National Plan for Teaching Swimming provides a guide for learn-to-swim schemes. It is not designed to be a series of structured lesson plans; the individual circumstances of each class, the ability of pupils in each class and the differing pool facilities make it difficult to be too prescriptive. However, the Plan, written by Hamilton Smith and John Lawton, does provide a developmental structure based on sound educational principles.

The Plan identifies the right level of performance for each aquatic skill and lays the foundation for core skills based on devoting time to what Smith and Lawton describe as the initial orientation of each pupil. Essentially this means that if time is devoted towards making pupils feel at ease with the water, so that they can balance and align their body correctly and be comfortable with early breathing techniques, they then have the right platform for the future, more complex skills.

Each phase of the Plan is tied into an ASA National Swim Award to incentivise the programme for pupils. The various stages are as follows:

- Foundation – Adult and child water activities
- Phase 1 – Non-swimmer: early confidence and movement skills
- Phase 2 – Beginner
- Phase 3 – Improver 1
- Phase 4 – Improver 2
- Phase 5 – Advanced 1
- Phase 6 – Advanced 2
- Phase 7 – Pre-competition

The National Plan, which has been in existence for about 8 years, is about to be revised.

Awarding and rewarding

Rewarding swimmers is important for a number of reasons:

- it provides an extra incentive for pupils to improve and to continue to improve
- it encourages parents to show an interest in their child's swimming
- it is a form of approval and recognition among peers.

Rewarding normally takes two forms: badges and certificates, and actions of approval. There are three types of award schemes: the ASA, the STA and the local authority. The various levels can vary from one local authority to another so a pupil moving to your school from another area may have been awarded a badge that does not relate to standards at your school. Both the ASA and STA provide national standards.

The ASA has a complete award scheme for all levels and types of swimmer. The awards that relate to the school swimming situation are the National Curriculum Water Skills Award and the National Curriculum Water Safety Award. The Water Skills Award comprises swimming 25 metres using a recognised stroke, treading water or floating unassisted for 30 seconds, and submerging the body underwater for a period of time. The ASA does, however, stress that this does not make pupils safe in deep water and that they should aim to improve from this point. In other words, this is the 'entry' point for swimming, not the 'end' point.

The National Curriculum Water Safety Award is an assessment in three sections: a question and answer sheet, work cards, and a practical test which can be land- or pool-based. Pupils are required to be able to:

- identify dangerous situations
- explain the dangers of water
- know how to behave near water
- identify the dangers to themselves
- identify the dangers in the local environment
- know how to summon assistance
- know how to access and respond while maintaining their own safety
- demonstrate on land or in the pool environment a reaching rescue
- demonstrate on land or in the pool environment a throwing rescue
- be able to identify other activities where the ability to swim is important
- explain the dangers of cold water.

The STA also offers a National Curriculum Award at Key Stage 2, supported by the International Swimming and Water Safety Standards Resource Manual.

The ASA has 12 separate awards under the title National Swim Awards. These are tied to the ASA National Plan for Teaching Swimming and are appropriate for primary school swimming pupils.

There are alternative ways of rewarding other than by badges and certificates. I like to call them 'actions of approval' and they can take the form of:

- recognition in school assemblies
- positive reinforcement on the return coach journey
- offering the opportunity for pupils to recount their achievements to other class members, either on the coach or back in the classroom
- end-of-term, internal, school awards ceremonies.

Carrying out your own risk assessment

Before running lessons at the pool, you should work through a series of simple questions to ensure that neither you nor the class are exposing yourselves to unnecessary risks. You have already considered plans for emergency action, but not all situations are immediate emergencies. There are a number of areas to consider. Of these, travel to and from the pool and the swimming lesson itself have already been covered (*see* pages 11–12 and 17–22). This section will look at the following:

- moving between the bus and the pool
- the process of changing
- teaching staff.

A general point is to visit the pool beforehand. Even if you have been to the pool many times before, it is always worth revisiting in order to make sure that things have not changed.

Moving between the bus and the pool

Most schools will travel to a public or school pool by bus, so determine where the bus will put down and pick up pupils. Points to consider are:

- to avoid, if possible, crossing roads, particularly main roads
- difficulty parking which can lead to pupils with damp hair waiting outside, sometimes in the winter
- if queuing needs to take place, this should be in the pool or school building
- the number of helpers and members of staff; you will have to give adequate cover if a situation arises where not all children will get on the bus at the same time.

The process of changing

The following should be borne in mind:

- Are pupils likely to be on their own in the changing rooms at any time?
- Who will supervise them during the changing process?
- Is there sufficient space for all pupils to dry down and change into their clothes? Lack of space can lead to pupils not drying adequately.
- Is the floor surface slippery? If it is slippery, determine what actions you will take.
- What other groups are likely to be in the changing rooms at the same time? What actions will you need to take to ensure that both your pupils and other changing room users have adequate space and use of facilities?

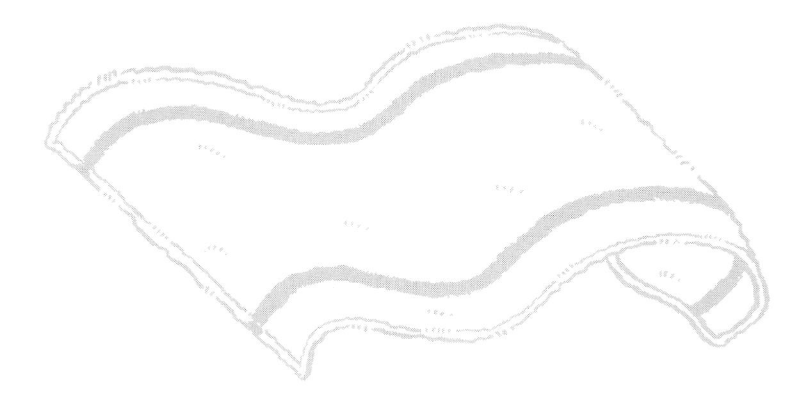

Teaching staff

In carrying out your own risk assessment, you should consider the following with all swimming teachers, school teachers and helpers involved with the visit:

- ❍ Do your swimming teaching staff have the right level of qualifications to teach the required size of group in the likely situation (*see* teaching qualifications, pages 22–25)?
- ❍ Fully consider the likely number of swimmers in each group and determine whether you have sufficient personnel with the right qualifications per head of participants.
- ❍ Decide what the roles of each staff member will be. Before the lessons, make sure that each member of staff and/or helper knows what is required of him/her in his/her role at the pool and what the legal position is for each person.
- ❍ How will you manage any disabled pupils or pupils with special needs?
- ❍ Check to ensure that the school has insurance to cover all personnel likely to be involved.
- ❍ Make sure that all teachers and helpers have been briefed on the ASA's guidelines on diving (see below).

Jumping into shallow water

While jumping and, later, diving, are important skills to teach, it is also essential that these skills are taught in a safe environment, and likely outcomes need to form part of your own risk assessment.

The ASA's guidance on performing a jumping entry states the following:

"Jumping into a swimming pool is an important skill which is invariably taught by swimming teachers and teachers of other aquatic disciplines. It needs to be recognised, however, that impact with the pool floor can result in injury to, for example, the ankles and lower spine. It is essential, therefore, that the activity is taught with care, taking into account the following factors:

- ❍ the depth of the water where the entry is being made
- ❍ the height of the freeboard (height of the pool side above the water)
- ❍ the size and weight of the pupil(s) making the entry
- ❍ age of the person making the entry (older people may suffer from brittle bones).

All those performing a jumping entry should be taught how to land correctly and how to recover themselves if overbalancing occurs. In addition, the importance of bending the knees on impact should be stressed.

Recommended minimum depth for jumping entries:

- ❍ Children who are water confident and in the early stages of learning to swim and normally up to 8 years of age: minimum depth 0.9 metres.
- ❍ Those children who are confident in deeper water (between 0.9–1.5 metres) and are normally aged 8 years plus, or adults in the early stage of learning to swim: minimum water depth should be at least level with the armpit of the individual when standing on the bottom of the pool."

(Source: *ASA Guidance/Information Document No.5*)

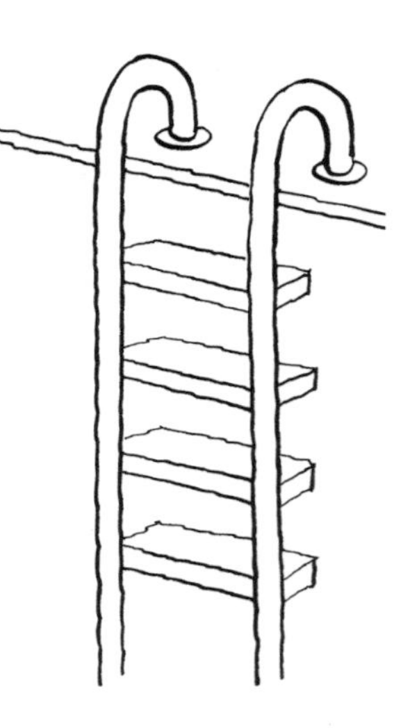

The above guidance relates to feet-first entries and not specific jumps which require the person involved to gain additional height from the pool side. In situations where this is required, a minimum depth of 1.8 metres is recommended."

Planning ahead

Your planning should be based on a number of factors:

- the standards and targets you set for the class
- the competencies of the class at the start of the year and what they have achieved in the past
- how many weekly lessons you plan for your class.

Medium- and long-term planning is normally carried out by the primary school's PE co-ordinator or swimming organiser; short-term planning on a lesson-by-lesson basis is carried out by the swimming or class teacher.

The Qualifications and Curriculum Authority (QCA) have established 33 Physical Education work schemes for pupils at Key Stages 1 and 2 (these can be accessed via the DfES Standards Site at www.standards.dfes.gov.uk). Two of these schemes are for swimming – one for Years 1, 2 and 3 (pitched at level 1) and one for Years 3, 4, 5 and 6 (pitched at level 4). These two lessons give an idea on how performance can be linked to assessment and this is important in planning for any scheme of work. Where the programme is being delivered by a pool operating company or a swimming teacher, the class teacher needs to liaise on targets, skills to be learnt, the anticipated outcomes and the process of managing these, as well as actions to be taken for the talented and gifted, the disabled and other disadvantaged groups. This is particularly the case if the class teacher is also required to act as a supporting swimming teacher.

CHAPTER 6

DfES CHARTER FOR SCHOOL SWIMMING

The Swimming Charter for school swimming was drawn up by the ASA and DfES in 2003 and was designed to draw on existing best practice.

Local authorities

The Charter considered that local authorities have an important part to play in delivering school swimming. In some places this includes service co-ordination, transport, pool access, swimming teacher training needs and timetabling advice to schools.

One of the important roles of local authorities in school swimming is to improve planning by assessing the users' future swimming needs. For school swimming, this can mean determining at what time of day different schools are likely to want to swim and the likely number of future swimmers. The Charter also encouraged local authorities to employ a dedicated swimming development manager to liaise with schools. Centralised management of school swimming is an effective way of delivering school swimming.

Schools

The Charter called on schools to:

- ensure that swimming forms part of the school's action planning, target setting and performance management process
- meet the class teachers' continuing professional development needs in order that teachers can deliver swimming either as a teacher or teaching assistant
- timetable swimming with cultural sensitivity
- consider combining resources with other schools to reduce costs
- work in partnerships, which may include block-booking lessons and transport.

Child protection issues

The Charter pointed out that everyone working with young people has a role to play in protecting them and safeguarding their welfare. Class teachers should, therefore, ensure that all adults working with their pupils have been cleared through official channels to work with children, and that all of these people are aware of child protection policies and procedures.

Class teachers should check to see that adults other than teachers and learning support staff have also been vetted to work with children. The Charter recommends that suitable supervision procedures are in place in changing areas.

CHAPTER 7

TOP-UP SWIMMING

What is top-up swimming? Quite simply, it is a short-term intervention designed to get pupils up to Key Stage 2 standard. This generally takes the form of lessons at the end of term but it can be used during or at the start of a new term. There are no set rules about how it should be delivered because the circumstances of each school will bring about different needs.

In 2002, I conducted pilot schemes on top-up swimming in Bristol and Durham for the DfES and ASA. Due to the relative success of the scheme, the DfES decided to fund a two-year programme of top-up swimming lessons.

The number of pupils who took part in the two pilot schemes was 828. This was equivalent to 19 per cent of pupils from the two local authority areas in Year 6 at that time. Following 10 consecutive days of concentrated half hour lessons, 51 per cent of the pupils in Durham and 68 per cent of the pupils in Bristol had reached the Key Stage 2 standard. Prior to the scheme, 19 per cent of all Year 6 pupils in both authorities could not reach the standard and the top-up scheme reduced this to 8 per cent. At first glance it might appear that, given the level of intensity, an 11 per cent improvement was not a great leap forward. But many of these pupils had difficulties in other areas – either in learning or socially. Given these difficulties, the results showed considerable improvement.

I spent some time researching reasons for pupils' inability to swim. The most important factors appeared to be family and school swimming cultures, or the lack of them. In many cases, pupils who lived nearest to a swimming pool never went swimming in their spare time. Teachers have a role to play in encouraging pupils to take part in swimming during their free time; this type of practice will contribute to improvement in their swimming ability. Time was also spent examining whether pupils from different cultural and economic backgrounds were more or less likely to be able to learn to swim. The pilot scheme found that pupils from minority groups were just as likely to be able to swim as those pupils from other backgrounds. Pupils from socially and economically disadvantaged backgrounds found it only slightly more difficult to learn to swim but, given the opportunity of taking part in lessons everyday, they were just as likely to improve at the same rate as the others.

The conclusion was that school swimming had an important role to play in offering pupils of all types the opportunity to swim and, for many pupils, it may be their only opportunity to learn. In the Top-Up Swimming Pilot Schemes Executive Summary, I comment: "Often success was accompanied by high emotions and feelings of pride and satisfaction from the young people. For many children, the true benefit of the scheme will long outlast the measurable benefits. The shared experience of achievement by teachers, children and their peers made this a key moment in their lives."

Organising top-up lessons

The main points to bear in mind with top-up swimming are:

- Plan ahead – decide what time of the year you plan to hold lessons and determine whether you wish to team up with other schools to make staffing and delivery easier.
- Decide at what point in the year you are going to determine which pupils are going to need top-up swimming. For example, if you are planning to deliver top-up swimming at the end of July, then you will probably need to decide by the end of May. You will then need to contact your local swimming pool to let them know the size of class they can expect, how many swimming teachers they will need to allocate and how much of the pool to set aside for the lessons.

- Early in the school year, you should contact your School Sport Partnership. The Partnership Development Manager is responsible for administering the budget and he/she needs to know that you are interested in taking part in order to set aside funds for your school.
- Encourage your local swimming pool to provide its most experienced swimming teacher.

The great strength of top-up swimming is that the classes are smaller and the lessons quieter. Pupils who have difficulty learning are often those most deterred by large classes, noise, splashing and the ability of others to learn more quickly. If possible, try to arrange for lesson times where there are no other groups in the learner's pool and when the pool is not likely to be overlooked by spectators.

Always bear in mind that top-up swimming is not a substitute for regular school swimming. Ten lessons over a short period can never replace regular and consistent lessons over the school year. In fact, some research has demonstrated that while a short-term period of swimming instruction will benefit pupils, unless it is supported by regular swimming over a longer period, it is quite likely that the skills learnt will be quickly forgotten. Top-up swimming should, therefore, be considered as a booster rather than a standard approach.

If you need to know more about top-up swimming, further information can be obtained by contacting the ASA's Customer Service Department on 0871 200 0928 or at customerservices@swimming.org.

CHAPTER 8

KEEPING RECORDS OF ACHIEVEMENT

The test sheets laid out on the next two pages show:

❍ a basic test recording sheet which is pitched at the level of the Key Stage 2 National Curriculum Standard (Table 2)

❍ a list of tests for a more advanced level (Table 3). This is a standard that all pupils transferring to secondary school should be able to achieve.

The main reasons for keeping records of attainment are:

❍ there is a requirement for records of attainment to be passed to secondary schools

❍ swimming could form part of an Ofsted inspection, and swimming forms part of the Physical Education component of the National Curriculum

❍ to determine, in conjunction with the ASA Regional Swimming Co-ordinators, which pupils will be required to take part in top-up swimming.

Administering the testing can be time-consuming if it is not well organised. Given that testing will take place towards the end of term, when there are likely to be many other demands on time, the whole process should be kept as straightforward as possible. The best approach is to have the class swimming teacher conducting the tests while you record the results.

The distance swimming takes up the bulk of the time and this can best be achieved by one pupil beginning his/her swim and the other group members following the first swimmer down the pool at five-second intervals. The swimmers should be asked to swim up one lane and back down the other in a rotational chain. Make sure you have a lifeguard specifically watching this activity as there will be a number of inexperienced swimmers extended to the maximum of their abilities at the same time. The lifeguard should position him/herself towards the deep end and ensure that he or she has a view of all the swimmers. Allow enough time after the distance swim for pupils to recover before the other activities – they will inevitably be tired!

Table 2

Recommended tests for class directed towards Key Stage 2						
School name:						
(Please tick box according to standard achieved or place a cross if standard not achieved at all)						
Pupil	Pupil	Pupil	Pupil	Pupil	Pupil	Pupil
Name						
Girl/Boy						
Test 1 – Swimming on front/back						
Under 10m						
11–24m						
25m Standard						
26–50m						
51–100m						
Test 2 – Floating on front						
0–5 sec						
6–10 sec						
11–20 sec						
21–30 sec						
Test 3 – Floating on back						
0–5 sec						
6–10 sec						
11–20 sec						
21–30 sec						
Test 4 – Treading water						
0–5 sec						
6–10 sec						
11–20 sec						
21–30 sec						
Test 5 – Sculling action						
Can scull						
Cannot scull						
Class-based course on water safety						
Work cards – passed						
Practical test – passed						
Answer sheet – passed						

Table 3

End-of-term tests – Advanced						
School name:						
(Please tick box according to standard achieved or place a cross if standard not achieved at all)						
Pupil	Pupil	Pupil	Pupil	Pupil	Pupil	Pupil
Name						
Girl/Boy						
Test 1 – Swimming on front						
Under 10m						
11–24m						
25m Standard						
26–50m						
51–100m						
100–200m						
Test 2 – Swimming on back						
Under 10m						
11–24m						
25m Standard						
26–50m						
51–100m						
100–200m						
Test 3 – Floating on front						
0–5 sec						
6–10 sec						
11–20 sec						
21–30 sec						
Test 4 – Floating on back						
0–5 sec						
6–10 sec						
11–20 sec						
21–30 sec						
Test 5 – Treading water						
0–5 sec						
6–10 sec						
11–20 sec						
21–30 sec						
Test 6 – Sculling action						
Can scull						
Cannot scull						

End-of-term tests – Advanced cont.						
School name:						
(Please tick box according to standard achieved or place a cross if standard not achieved at all)						
Pupil	Pupil	Pupil	Pupil	Pupil	Pupil	Pupil
Name						
Girl/Boy						
Test 7 – Put head underwater						
0–5 sec						
6–10 sec						
11–20 sec						
Test 8 – Jump into water						
Yes						
No						
Test 9 – Surface dive						
Yes						
No						
Test 10 – Breaststroke movements						
Yes						
No						
Class-based course on water safety						
Work cards – passed						
Practical test – passed						
Answer sheet – passed						

Key skills for recording

Let's imagine that this is the first time you have had to administer any testing for swimming and you have very little experience to draw on. What would be the main elements to look out for? In general, there are five key components and these can all be assessed to some degree. They are as follows:

- *Body position* – the main consideration is whether the body position is flat to the surface of the water. As one example, is the head held too high? Does this affect the overall body position?
- *Leg kick* – you need to consider whether the leg kick is systematic and rhythmic, and whether it contributes to overall propulsion and balance. If the legs are too low, they will increase drag; if they are too high, the feet may break the surface excessively and retard progress in a different way.
- *Arm action* – there can be many problems with the arm technique but check that the hands are entering the water at the start of the stroke in the right position, e.g. on front crawl and backstroke, are the hands entering in line with the shoulders? Do the arms recover smoothly and effectively or do they spoil the overall balance of the stroke?
- *Breathing* – this is probably the most important stroke attribute. It takes considerable practice to carry it out efficiently. Watch out for whether the pupil is breathing out once on every stroke. If this is not taking place, it will contribute to increased fatigue.
- *Timing* – there are a number of ways of timing the arms and legs; all are correct providing the stroke is moving the body forward. There are, however, some stroke timings that are considerably better than others. The timing needs to suit the individual and the key question to ask yourself is whether the particular timing carried out by the pupil being assessed contributes to the stroke being continuously propulsive.

Testing can take two forms. First, it can be the type of test which takes place from one swimming lesson to another. This is sometimes called diagnostic assessment. The second is summative assessment, which is made at the end of each Key Stage. It should be noted that there is no statutory requirement on the part of teachers to record and report pupils' performance based on the level descriptions at Key Stages 1 and 2.

CHAPTER 9

LINKS FROM SCHOOL SWIMMING

Planning the transition for pupils from primary to secondary schools

Many teachers in England may not realise that there is a statutory requirement for schools to have assessed and recorded pupils' level of attainment in relation to the targets at Key Stage 2. These records should be made available to each pupil's new secondary school. This is slightly different in Wales, where the standards are not the same. For instance, there is no requirement to swim 25 metres as there is in England. In Scotland, there is no swimming entitlement for school pupils.

The handover from primary to secondary school requires a little more than just the immediate record keeping for each pupil. In order to help secondary schools, any gifted and talented pupils should be highlighted and any pupils that are already members of swimming clubs noted. Importantly, attention should also be drawn to any pupils that have not reached the Key Stage 2 standard, particularly those that cannot achieve the basic standard of swimming 25 metres. Those pupils that have not achieved the 25-metre standard are at risk if they take part in other water-based sports at secondary school level, and they should continue to have lessons either at school or out of school to achieve this minimum standard and thereby avoid being exposed to any danger from water.

If you have pupils that have not achieved this standard, they will either be able to attend extra top-up lessons now being provided by the DfES, or they should be encouraged to take part in summer intensive courses at their local pool, or swim with their parents at the pool.

Club–school links opportunities

The aim behind the club–school links opportunities is to increase pupils' access to swimming provision, and for more children to participate regularly in swimming activity as part of a healthy lifestyle beyond the curriculum. Launched in 2002, it was designed so that schools and clubs could work together to create pathways for pupils that will keep them swimming.

Pupils should be able to balance their commitments between school and clubs and should understand how they complement each other. The links should offer pupils the opportunity to take part in a range of related activities so that if they want to specialise later on in their lives, they are able to do so.

The aim has been to create a national infrastructure for PE and school sport by developing 400 specialist sports colleges and School Sport Co-ordinator Partnerships by 2006. Also, by 2006, there will be 800 accredited clubs with links that have been established with schools. The aim is to have linked 60,000 pupils between the ages of 5 and 16 years.

In addition, there is a programme for the gifted and talented which will encourage pupils to join junior sports clubs. These are being aided by talent development camps for pupils in Years 6 and 7. 'Step into sport' is a further strand which encourages young people to become involved in volunteering to help in sport.

For swimming, there are a range of ideas. These include:

- an interactive teaching tool kit for pupils, teachers and parents, designed to increase understanding of swimming and water safety
- the Swimming Charter
- the top-up pilot scheme and a linked web site.

Details of where to access the information listed above can be found on pages 93–96.

Summer- or holiday-time swimming schemes for pupils

We all recognise that swimming has a role to play in introducing many young people to water. Teachers should advise pupils that this swimming can, and indeed should, be supplemented by further practice. Often pupils will not know how to start taking this practice and school teachers will need to provide guidance.

There are three main ways of continuing to practice:

- Through admission to unstructured swimming sessions at the local swimming pool. The best time of the day for a pupil to attend is during the holiday periods and pupils should be encouraged to try to go when there is no other programmed activity.
- Through a structured learn to swim programme. Here, it is important that teachers advise the parents as to the benefits. Parents should be encouraged to book these lessons well in advance. For example, in the summer, intensive courses are hard to get on to and can carry a minimum waiting time of anything up to six months.
- Another low-cost way of achieving this practice is through free swimming initiatives. Many local authorities are staging free swimming, often in the school holidays, in the belief that pool admission prices are a barrier to participation in swimming. Free swimming is an interventionist procedure designed to bring about social and behavioural change. Class teachers should be aware of the opportunities in order to inform their pupils when free swimming is taking place in their area.

Increasingly, free tuition is being offered with free swimming as a way of reducing attrition in these initiatives. Some local authorities were finding that people were losing interest after one or two swims and they have introduced a stronger educative element to combat this. The time to find out about free swimming initiatives is when you are initially booking the pool for school swimming lessons. School Sport Partnerships should also be in a position to inform all 'family schools'.

The key factor in free swimming is that it provides children from lower-income families with an opportunity to swim. Parents in a better economic position can afford to pay for private swimming lessons for their children. It is worth pointing out to students that the afternoon sessions during free swimming initiatives are quieter. Due to their high popularity, free swimming days are often now extremely busy. Many free swimming initiatives last only for a short time.

CHAPTER 10

PERSONAL SWIMMING EQUIPMENT

Personal equipment is often a matter of choice but there are a few useful house rules for the class teacher to follow. Many of these are common sense.

It is worth dressing for the job. Often, what you wear on the pool side will give a message to the class as well as to the people around you. The first factor to bear in mind is that indoor pools are almost invariably warm atmospheres for anyone wearing outdoor clothes. A lightweight polo shirt is more practical than a dressier shirt. Training shoes are preferable to bare feet and these shoes should be non-slip and as waterproof as possible.

A whistle is a useful addition but make sure it is strung around the neck so that in an emergency you can get to it quickly without struggling to find it in your pocket. Where class testing is taking place, always take a clipboard with pen.

Spare kit for teachers

Where goggles are allowed in class, it is useful to have a spare pair in case a pupil breaks his or her goggles during the lesson. Similarly, it is worth having a couple of spare swimming caps available.

A set of new ear plugs and a nose clip are other pieces of equipment that are useful to have with you. Also, take spare, ready-washed swimwear which is of the appropriate size for your pupils. It might also be a good idea to take a clean towel in case a pupil forgets his or her own towel. All of the above can fit neatly into one kit bag.

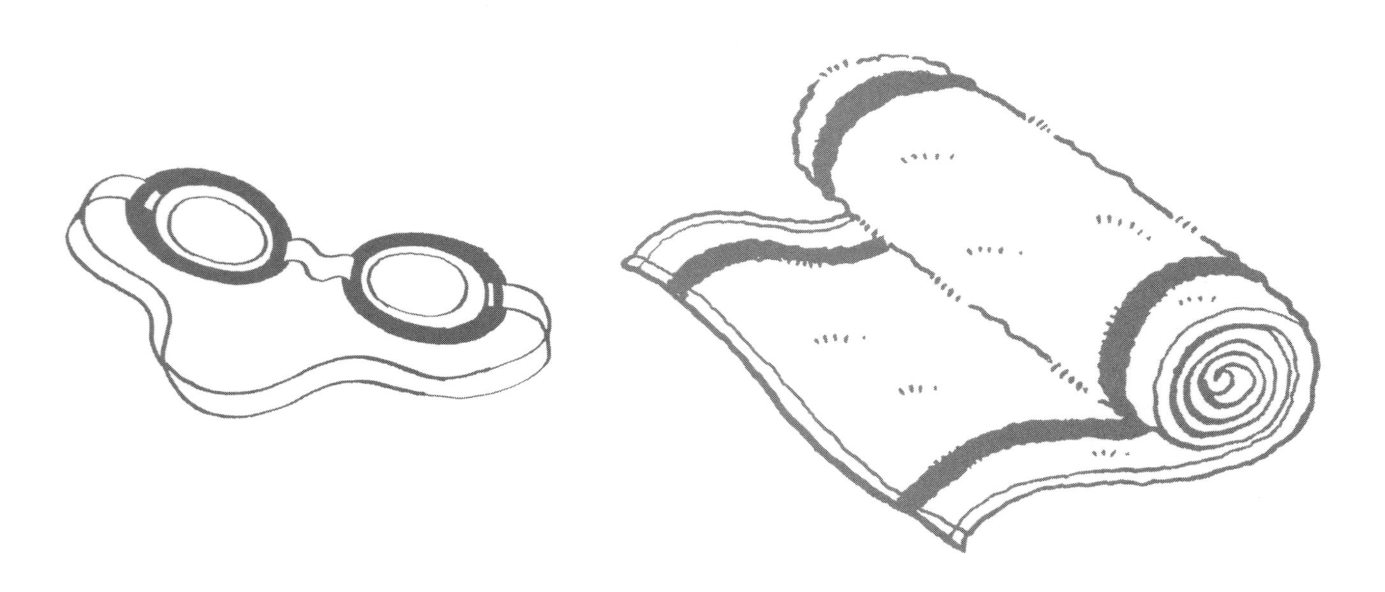

Arm bands

Some teachers prefer to teach without the use of arm bands. I don't necessarily want to be an advocate for their use, but school teachers with large classes of pupils might want to employ them, particularly if the class has learners in relatively deep water.

Always make sure the arm bands are inflated before arriving at the pool and this means carrying them in a large plastic bag. There is generally insufficient time to blow up arm bands as well as supervising class changing prior to the lesson.

The arm bands should be an appropriate size for each pupil and should not be blown up to such an extent that they are uncomfortable or take a considerable amount of time to put on. Always make sure that pupils wearing arm bands are both accessible from the pool side and can stand on the bottom. Pupils in arm bands in deep water are a hazard.

Wearing suitable swimwear

Before taking a class to the pool, it is advisable to brief pupils on the type of swimwear you expect them to wear. The wrong type of swimwear can be dangerous to learners and can hamper the learning process. Bermuda shorts are great for relaxing on the beach on holiday but they tend to be made of material which clings to the legs and is, therefore, less conducive to the learning situation.

Other types of costumes to be avoided are those that trap air or water and/or rub under the arms. Pupils need to ensure that they avoid swimwear that is difficult to tie at the waist. Two-piece costumes for girls are also unsuitable for learning. You might want to take some time on the bus to explain that the life of a swimsuit can be increased by washing it out in clean tap water after use. This will help to remove pool chemicals and other pollutants.

Some faith groups require the body to be fully covered at a swimming pool so some parents make their own costumes in order to allow their children to take part in swimming. In some places, parents have sewn together pyjamas because they were both light and did not trap too much air.

Among other considerations, jewellery and any other items hanging from the body can make the learning situation more dangerous.

Safer ways of wearing goggles

Before the start of the first lesson, determine whether the pool management and the local education authority have a specific policy towards goggles. Goggles may be forbidden, so it is worth finding out before the first lesson. In general, it is probably better not to encourage goggles unless there is a specific medical reason for wearing them. They are valuable swimming aids but they can also distract pupils in an early learning situation.

If goggles do need to be worn due to medical or other reasons, it is vital that pupils are taught the correct way of putting them on. This is best achieved by first of all placing the eye pieces securely over the eye sockets and then, while holding the eye pieces tight (but not too tight) to the eye sockets, the pupil should ease the strap over the apex and down the back of the head so that the goggles are secure. Pupils should avoid pulling the eye pieces away from the eye sockets when adjusting or putting the goggles on. If the goggles were to break, or the pupil was to allow the eye pieces to spring back, it would cause an accident.

Pool-side equipment

Most pools will provide the basic equipment used for teaching swimming. If these items are not supplied, then you should think of taking the following to the pool:

- *Floats* – small polystyrene floats are useful for leg practice and for building up kicking strength as well as skills.
- *Arm bands* – as mentioned above, these aid independent movement at an early stage and help to build confidence.
- *Hoops and bricks* – designed to encourage swimming underwater.

Generally, the above will be supplied. Normally a pool will provide pool dividers which will enable pupils to be divided up from other pool users.

You may want to purchase the following because these are unlikely to be supplied by pools:

- *Woggles and noodles* – these are useful alternative pieces of equipment for flotation support when learning.
- *Egg flips* – these can be used to encourage pupils to breathe through the mouth on, and just under, the surface of the water.
- *Buoyancy suits* – a few pools may have these to hand. They are designed to bring the pupil to a more horizontal learning position.

PART 2
THE PRACTICE

CHAPTER 11

BASIC SWIMMING TEACHING TECHNIQUES

Getting in and out of the water

The first experience of getting into the water in a swimming pool can be both exhilarating and frightening. The teacher, therefore, has a responsibility to make it as safe and positive an experience as possible. If there are steps at the shallow end of the pool, ask the class to climb backwards down the steps into the water. This should be done pupil by pupil. Get pupils to fix their eyes on the steps in front of them in order to keep the body upright and avoid leaning back too far. Also, they should hold the sides of the steps firmly but not too tensely with their hands.

Where there are no steps at the shallow end, and in situations where the depth of the water will make it possible for pupils to stand, ask the class to sit over the side of the pool. Tell pupils to kick and splash the water with their feet in order to get a feel for it. Ask the class to start by placing their hands on the ground either side of their hips. Then move the right hand across the front of the stomach and place it on the ground so that it faces in the opposite direction to the left. At this point the hands should be adjacent to one another. Placing the weight of the right arm on to the right hand, pupils should now twist the body so that the face looks inwards towards the wall. This will have the effect of turning the rest of the body which can now be steadily lowered into the water.

Moving around

As soon as your class has entered the pool, pupils should be encouraged to get to know the water and to move freely about the shallow end or learners' pool. Tell them to walk around very carefully by keeping their shoulders on the surface, balancing with their hands in the water and keeping their eyes fixed in front of them.

You may want to be more gradual in this introduction by getting the class to hold the pool side or rail first and getting them to move along it. They can start gradually, by sliding their feet along the bottom, but eventually they can start to bob up and down. Other variations include getting pupils to:

- move freely on an unstructured basis
- change direction slowly and then rapidly
- follow the shape of a rectangle or triangle on the bottom
- try transferring their weight from one foot to the other and working on different variations with their feet, such as hopping and jumping with two feet forwards and backwards.

Becoming acquainted with the water

Now encourage the class to try a few more familiarity practices, including:

- washing the face
- taking handfuls of water and spooning it on to the back of the head
- jumping lightly up and down while the hands are holding the side of the pool in front, eventually moving to a 'jack in the box' motion
- placing the arms outstretched on the surface and pulling the hands from side to side in sweeping motions

- lowering the face and blowing bubbles (this can be done with table tennis balls)
- placing toys on the bottom of the pool then getting pupils to reach down and bring them to the surface, or getting pupils to touch the bottom of the pool.

Getting the feet off the bottom

Once pupils get past the stage of bobbing off the bottom by either walking round the pool or by holding the pool side, there are several other activities you can carry out to develop confidence levels. These are as follows:

- Pupils hold the rail or pool side and draw the knees up.
- Pupils hold the side and push lightly off the bottom, pointing their toes so that the legs drift to the centre.
- The above can be followed by getting pupils to put their face in the water.
- Pupils hold the side and kick the legs alternately by stretching their legs out behind and shaking their feet.
- The above, but asking pupils to try different ways of kicking, for example, by splashing as much as possible with the feet right on the surface and then by kicking as deep as possible to feel the resistance of the water.

Learning to float

A simple starting point is to get pupils to take two floats, placing one under each armpit and wrapping the arms over the top of each float. Ask the class to lift their feet off the bottom by bending the knees slightly while keeping the shoulders on the surface of the water. They should pull their knees up to their chest. The aim is to keep the feet up as long as they can. This should be repeated a few times with a view to keeping the feet off the ground for a little longer each time.

The use of two floats provides additional support. Later, pupils can move on to mush-room-and star-shaped floats. Once sufficient confidence has been gained, ask the class to split up into pairs. Using one float, one partner will then stand on the bottom holding one end of the float. The other end of the float is held by the other pupil, who stretches out on his or her front, pointing the toes and keeping the elbows straight. The 'carrying' pupil can then walk very slowly backwards while the 'floating' pupil attempts to kick his or her legs lightly. Eventually, many different types of shape can be tried – on the front, side and back both with arms and legs together and apart, or with limbs wrapped and flexed.

Submerging the face

Many teachers recommend teaching the breathing technique by getting the face underwater at home. This can be done with a bowl of water.

Submerging the face should be introduced cautiously in the class situation. An explanation of breathing is given later in the front crawl section (*see* pages 60–61). Caution should be employed because it forms one of the three great initial experiences – entering the water, floating for the first time and submerging – and the type of experience in these three activities can determine whether pupils keep swimming.

Here are a few ways to start:

- Hold the rail or pool side and blow bubbles through the mouth.
- Feel the way down the pool side by placing the hands on the wall and moving down the pool a little further each time. Stress the importance of keeping the fingers in touch with the wall and mention that the face will eventually go under.
- Count a partner's fingers under the water while standing or crouching alongside the pool wall.

- Bobbing in pairs – pupils hold hands and one partner bends his/her knees and takes a breath prior to sinking under the water. After blowing out air under the water, he/she returns to the surface and the other partner tries the same movement.

Eventually, pupils can move away from the pool edge and attempt to:

- continue to count fingers underwater
- submerge and blow bubbles at one another
- duck under and come up through hoops (but this will take a number of sessions before sufficient confidence is reached).

Sculling

Learning to make free-form shapes in water should be preceded by sculling – floating without the use of buoyancy aids. This is the follow-on for pupils who have learnt to float with two floats, one under each arm. The hands should be stretched out at the sides with the palms facing down towards the bottom of the pool. Pupils should now make flat figures of eight with the hands. The feet are lifted from the bottom at the same time. The upright floating position is now supported by this figure-of-eight movement. Using sculling movements, the body can float in a number of different positions.

Games in the water

Water games can be a useful tool. They both encourage enjoyment and distract pupils from their fears. Games can be divided into two types – first, those that encourage movement around the pool, and second, those that are slightly more advanced and can make a useful contrasting activity towards the end of a lesson which has required a considerable amount of concentrated learning. Many of these games will be familiar because they are used on dry land, in the playground and during PE lessons.

Games to encourage moving around a pool

- Simon says
- All common types of tag games
- Moving an 'egg flip' around the pool by blowing it
- Walking races across the widths
- Zig zag around other class members acting as statues
- Pushing a ball with the nose (and later, with the inside of the arms)
- Copying what your partner is doing
- Mirroring what your partner is doing
- On the whistle, moving to different parts of the pool
- Dodging around the pool in pairs; one pupil tries to avoid the other
- Moving from ship to shore on command
- Retrieving objects from different parts of the pool
- Walking swim – the class crouches and moves around the pool following one another in a circle by mimicking front crawl movement while walking

Games that can be used as a contrasting or alternative activity

- *Over and under* – the class breaks up into teams. Each team stands in the water about a metre apart. The pupil at the end of the row works his or her way to the front of the row, jumping over and under alternate standing pupils.
- *Alternate duck* – the class is split into groups which stand in a circle holding hands. Each alternate pupil lowers his/her head and face into the water while the others stay on the surface.
- *Volleyball* – a rope can be strung from one side of the pool to the other. Pupils stand on the bottom and mimic volleyball. Only one ball is used for the game.
- *Obstacle courses* – the class can work its way round the pool trying to overcome various tests, for example, ducking under hoops and balancing light objects on the head while walking.
- *Traffic lights* – the class moves around the pool responding to red, orange and green colours held up by the teacher.
- *Two dogs and a bone* – pupils face one another in the pool about two metres apart. Their task is to grasp an object placed halfway between them. They are challenged to carry the object back to the pool side without being tagged.
- *Treading water tag* – the class treads water; if a pupil stops treading water, he or she can be tagged.
- *Treasure hunt* – a variety of teaching aids and toys are thrown into the pool. From the pool side, pupils retrieve as many objects as possible. These objects can be lying on the bottom or on the surface of the pool.
- *Musical statues* – pupils move around the pool. When the music stops, they must 'freeze'.
- *Dive and collect relay* – similar to the treasure hunt but competing between teams.
- *Musical hoola hoops* – hoops float on the surface and when the music stops, each pupil tries to submerge into a hoop.
- *Poison* – the class forms into circles by holding hands. The circles move round and pupils attempt to pull others in their circle into a large object which represents the poison.
- *Number retrieve* – pupils form a circle in the water and are given a number. When a sinking object is thrown into the middle of the circle and a number is called out, the relevant pupil has to retrieve the object.
- *Floating pond* – on the teacher's command, the whole pool should be floating using any shape. They should hold their position until the teacher blows a whistle or uses an alternative command.

Positioning on the pool side

Whether you are a school teacher acting as the lead teacher with a class or a swimming teacher, there are several points to bear in mind:

- Make sure you can be seen by all the class without class members placing themselves in unnecessary danger at the pool.
- Ensure that you adopt a position where you can be heard by the whole class. You should avoid standing where the pool roof is low or where there are too many walls surrounding you.
- Make sure that the class members know beforehand what the signal is when they should stop whatever they are doing and be prepared to listen to you.

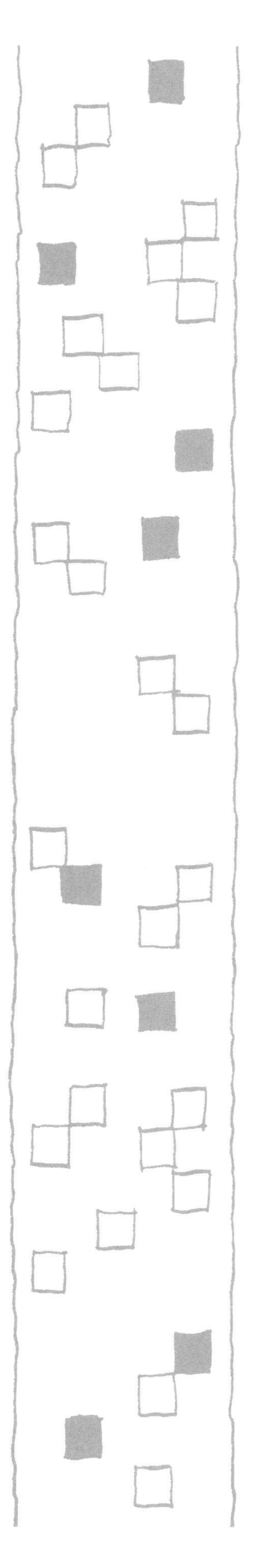

- If you have weaker swimmers in your class or group, avoid stopping the class when they are in the middle of the deep end or where it is necessary to keep swimming or floating because they are out of their depth.

The class or swimming teacher should not be in the pool with pupils unless there are enough qualified swimming teachers present to ensure that there is sufficient cover on the pool side.

With regard to positioning, there are three main factors to consider:

- pupils' safety
- pupils' ability to receive instruction
- pupils' position in the water in relation to the tasks they are being asked to carry out.

You should always give instructions or talk to the group as a whole from a position where you can see all pupils all of the time, and at the same time. Often this will be by positioning yourself at the end of a line.

When you are asking a pupil in the water to demonstrate a skill, get the rest of the class to sit, stand or hold the pool side. Make sure you speak to the class from a position where you can see all of your pupils and the demonstrator during the demonstration.

Figures 2 to 4 are examples of good practice in positioning. This is by no means an exhaustive reference but will serve as a guide.

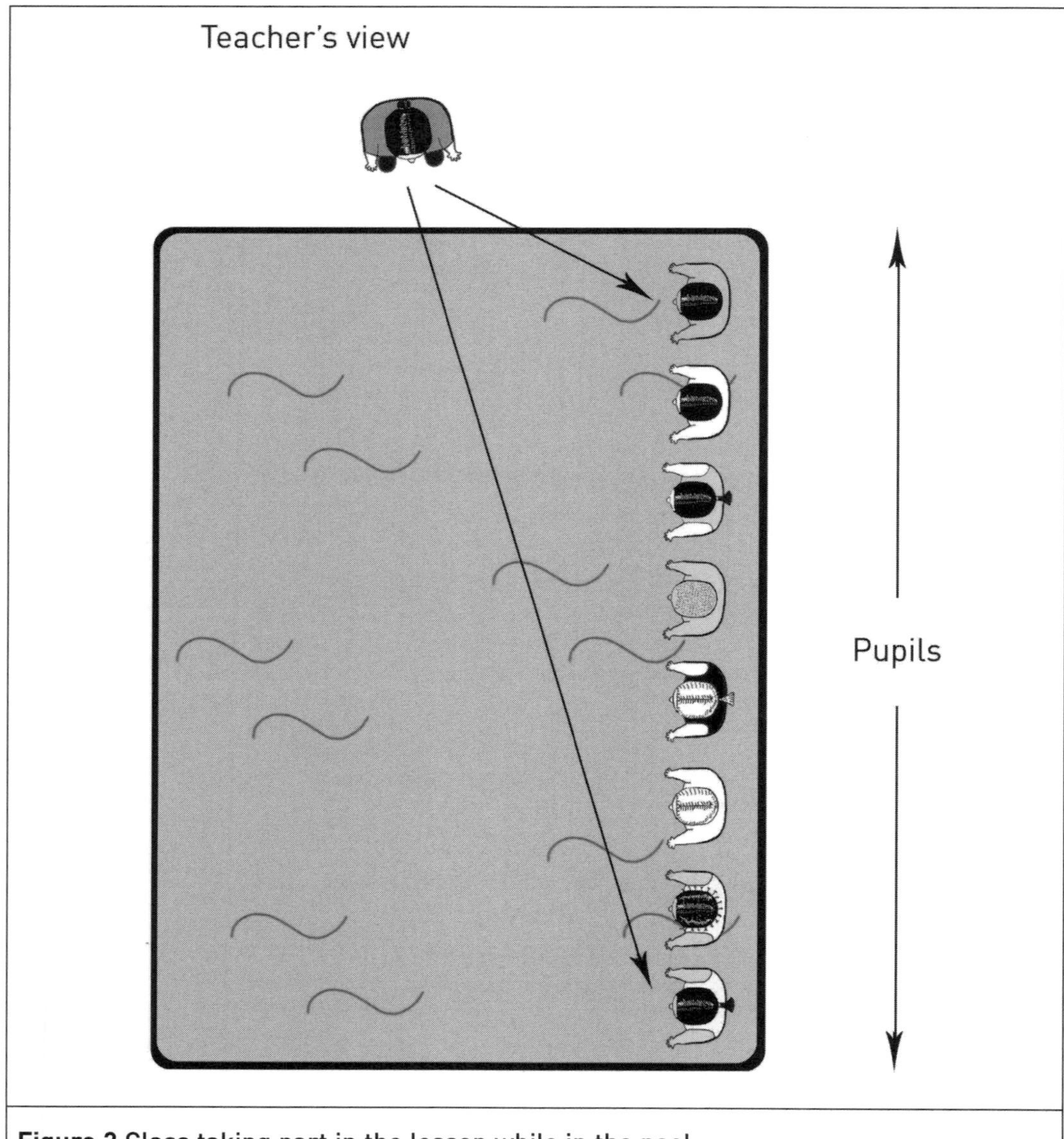

Figure 2 Class taking part in the lesson while in the pool

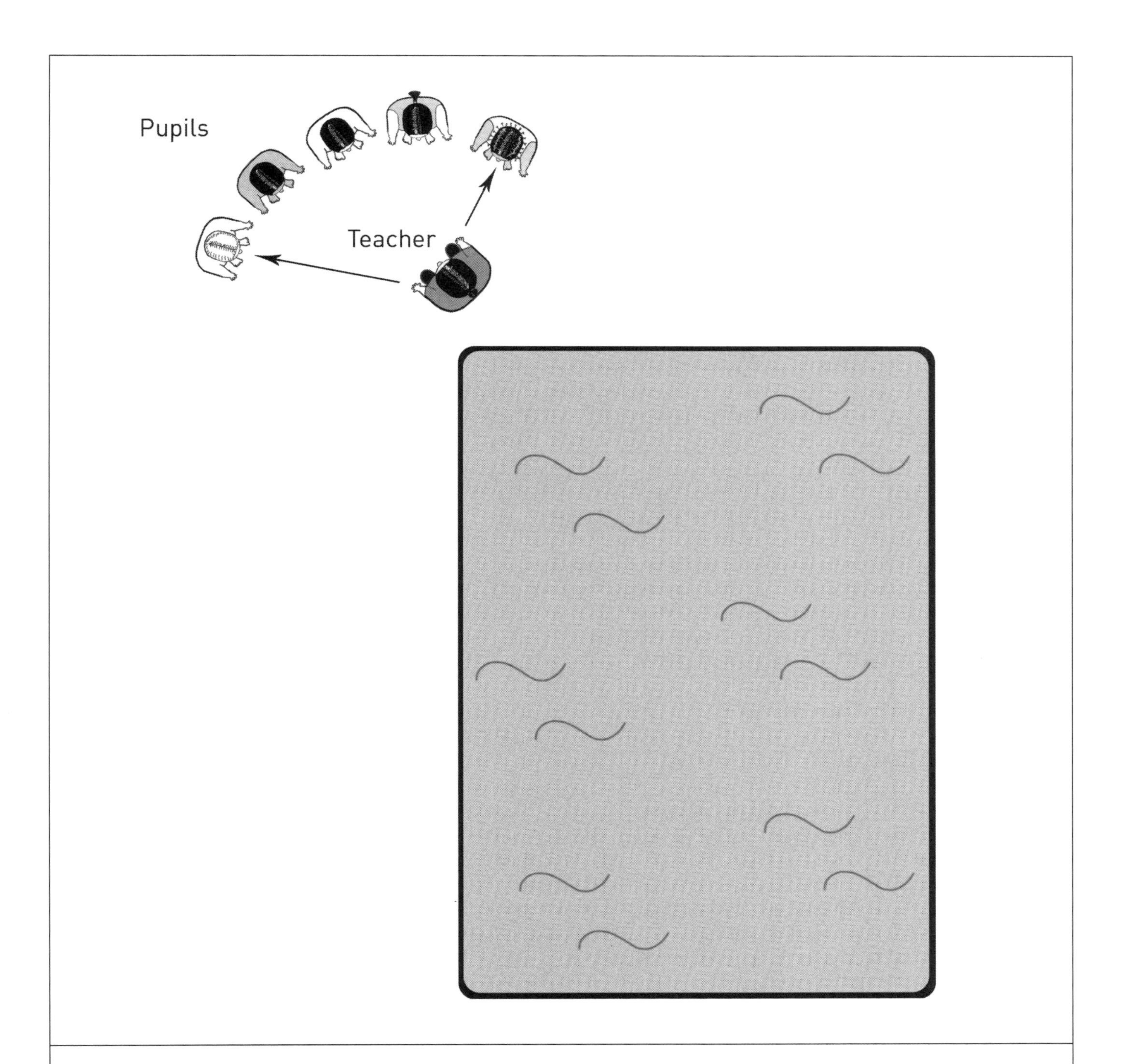

Figure 3 Class and teacher on the pool side for teaching

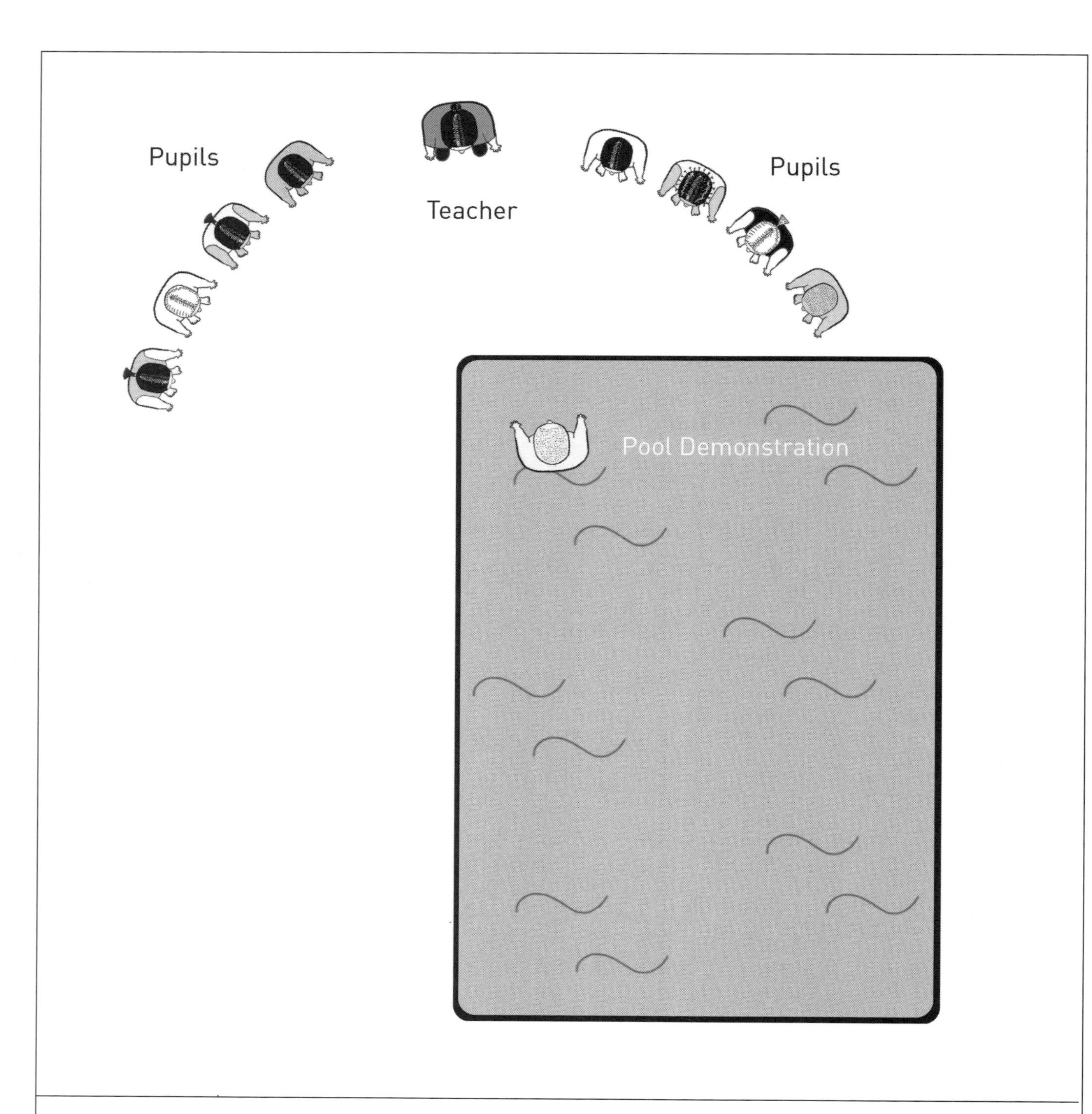

Figure 4 With demonstration in pool

Overcoming language barriers

The UK's increasingly multicultural society now means that English is often a second language. Sometimes, a whole class may have insufficient language skills and pupils may find it difficult to hear or comprehend what is taking place at the pool.

Quite often this problem is overcome by pupils copying other pupils and by the teacher demonstrating what is expected of them. However, swimming pools are difficult places to hear instructions and class teachers should consider taking an additional adult who can translate where necessary.

If you are confronted with this situation, explain each item in English first and then get a translator to give your instructions in the predominant language. Finally, follow this by getting a pupil that understands English to demonstrate the required skill in the water. Where this is not possible, demonstrate the skills with your own hands and body on the pool side. Let pupils try the skill once, then blow your whistle and reiterate the main components of the skill shortly after they have tried the skill for the first time. Reinforcement of the visual is of great value.

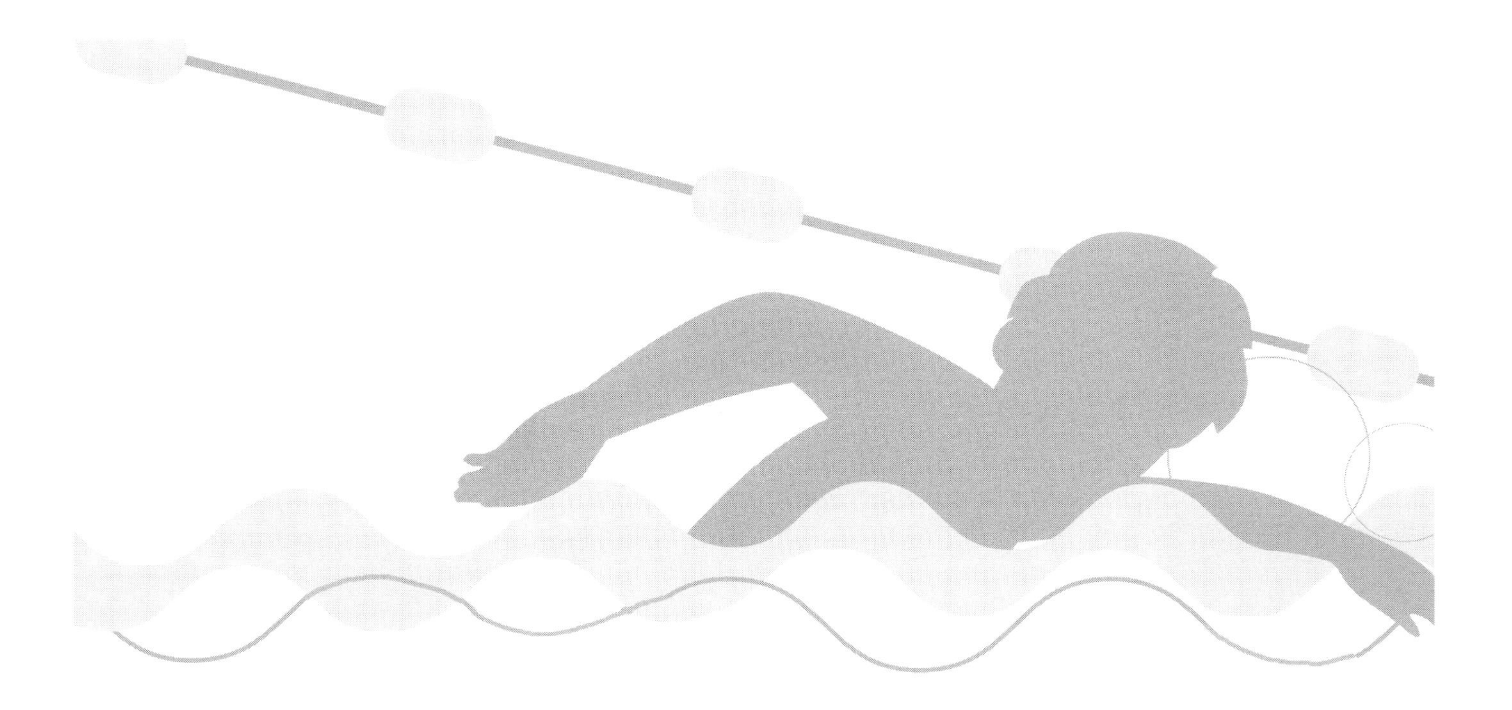

CHAPTER 12

NEXT STAGES

Dog paddle

Dog paddle is a good starting stroke. As pupils do not have to recover the arms over the water, they are likely, at this early stage, to be more balanced in the water as well as encountering less resistance.

Dog paddle is best learnt through kicking legs and holding a float. The early stages of kicking with a float can be difficult. Controlling the float and moving forward can cause initial problems. Occasionally, you will find that some pupils tend to go backwards when they kick. It takes practice to get the body in a position where the legs can kick to give propulsion.

Get the class to hold a float each and stand in the shallow part of the water. Hold the float at one end so that the thumbs are positioned on top and the palms face in towards the float itself. Then ask the class to kneel in the water or crouch to lower the shoulders to the level of the surface of the water. The arms should now be stretched out in front and pupils should very gently push, either with the knees or the feet, off the bottom, so as to straighten the body along the surface.

If the class is comfortable and can balance, try this again but stretching out further. If pupils are not confident with this, get them to start by kneeling on the bottom and encourage them simply to stretch the feet backwards without pushing the body forwards. The best way to achieve this is by initially lifting the knees off the bottom and by feeling water pressure on them. Then ask the class to put their knees or feet back on the bottom. They should try lifting the knees until they are confident enough to point the toes. Once this has been achieved, they will be able to glide forward in a more balanced manner.

The next stage is to get the class to start to kick by pointing the toes and then straightening the knees. Teaching points should be to get them to shake the feet as well as point the toes, so that the ankles are loose and relaxed. The power of the kick should come from the upper leg.

Once the legs have been mastered, get the class to stretch the fingers and move the arms in a dog-like swimming manner. Ask the class to straighten the arms at the elbows on the recovery, i.e. when the arms stretch out in front of the face under the water. Encourage pupils to pull with their hands and forearms, not just with the hands. The pull should continue back to the stomach and then recover forward again. The stroke can be swum with the head up at first and then, later, when pupils are more confident, they can swim with the head down and eyes fixed on the bottom of the pool.

Kicking on the back

Generally, it is easier to start pupils on their front, but occasionally a pupil will feel more comfortable on his or her back. As a rule, attempt to teach the rudimentary basics for dog paddle before attempting backstroke movements, but in cases where you get a pupil that prefers the back, do not discourage him or her. Some pupils prefer swimming on the back at first because they are fearful of putting their face in or near water. At the initial stages, the important factor is to encourage pupils in techniques where they are comfortable.

Try to teach backstroke legs in a shallow water area. Start with the class kneeling in the water or standing with the knees bent, so that the shoulders are down on the surface. From this position, pupils can quickly get to the correct position without creating too much turbulence close to the surface.

Next, instruct pupils to place the head so that the middle section of the back of the head rests on the surface of the water. You should explain that the aim is to avoid any strain on the neck with the weight of the head being carried by the water. Tell pupils that when they can feel the weight of the head being carried by the water, to bring their knees up to the surface and point their toes. Run through this practice several times until the class is more confident.

Now that pupils can balance more easily, the leg action can be introduced.

Teaching points

- Throughout the kick, stress the importance of blowing out through the mouth more than breathing in.
- The leg kick should be made from the hips in an alternating up and down movement.
- The recovery, or down, kick should descend until the feet hang diagonally from the knees towards the bottom. Meanwhile, the other leg should be pointed at the toes with the knee extended as it drives upwards.

Inform the class that the kick should be strong but only the toes should break the surface. Suggest that pupils imagine that they are trying to kick a football off the surface aiming for a point about 30 centimetres above the surface. The knees should not bend on the up kick and should stay under the surface. At the same time, the ankles should remain loose on the down kick and flexible on the up kick. This will help to achieve a whipping movement.

You may find that there are pupils who are still not confident about floating or kicking on their back. If this is the case, get them to float with a buoyancy aid under each arm. Tell pupils to wrap their lower arms over the floats in order to provide greater buoyancy. The best way is for the arms to be held out straight at either side. This helps to stabilise the pupil's body around the shoulder joint. Another method is to encourage pupils to carry a float behind the head. From a technical perspective, this tends to make it difficult to adopt a good head position during the next stages. To avoid this, it is better to hold one float in both hands with the arms held out straight, so that the float rests over the pelvic girdle on the surface. Slowly, the pupil will become more confident and you can encourage him or her to adjust the head and be more streamlined by tucking in the chin and looking slightly towards the feet.

Star and mushroom floats

The star and mushroom floats are fairly simple skills that can be used in class swimming lessons as a contrasting activity.

For the mushroom float, ask the class to stand on the bottom of the pool in shallow water. Then ask pupils to lift their knees to their chest and to wrap their arms around the front of their shins. At first, pupils will probably try to do this while keeping their face above the water. Later, they should be encouraged to take a large breath prior to taking their feet off the bottom. They can then place their chin on their chest while lifting their knees up. They should aim to be bobbing on the water. The overall effect is to create a human ball with the eyes facing down towards the bottom of the pool.

The star float is the reverse. Instead of pulling the body together in a ball, pupils should aim to open their bodies out to a maximum. Encourage them to mimic a flower opening in the spring. Pupils should be asked to bend their knees and push off from a standing position by extending the knees and pushing down on the soles of the feet. The arms should be extended in line with the shoulders, with the palms of the hands facing down towards the surface of the water. As they push down on the bottom of the pool, pupils should be asked to point their toes and part their legs to their maximum. The overall effect is a face-down star shape in the water. As with the mushroom float, pupils will probably start by performing this water skill with their heads above water. Eventually, they should be encouraged to take a breath and place their faces in the water. While exhaling, they should face down to the bottom of the pool to make the shape as aesthetic as possible.

CHAPTER 13

ADVANCED STROKES

At primary school level, the target should be for all pupils to be able to swim freestyle, backstroke and breaststroke. Breaststroke is technically a more difficult stroke to master so, as a minimum, pupils should have an awareness of, and have, attempted co-ordinated breaststroke movements. This chapter explains how these strokes should be swum and a typical teaching sequence for each of them.

Freestyle

Freestyle is also known as front crawl. You should be looking to build on the dog paddle that you have already taught to the class. The essential difference between dog paddle and freestyle is that the arms are recovered over the water. This is achieved by lifting the arm out of the water when it has finished pulling just beyond the hips. The thumb should point towards the side of the body as the hand is lifted out.

Get the class to go through the arm movement on the side of the pool. The arms should operate alternately by bending the elbows when the hands go past the hips. This will enable the hands to be lifted forwards and placed into an imaginary water surface in front of the head.

Now ask the class to get into the water and to try the movement while standing and crouching forward in the water. Get pupils to push off from the side and to try to move their arms over the water with the head in and looking immediately in front. Encourage the class to go as far as they can on one breath. This will get them to pull with their arms without interruption. As when practising on the pool side, pupils should be encouraged to bend the elbows when recovering the arms over the water.

Getting the breathing right is important; it forms a big part of the overall co-ordination of the stroke. Ask the class to hold the rail or side of the pool. Most learners have difficulty in balancing the pressure of air inside the nose with the pressure of water outside it. The best idea is to get pupils to stand and place their face in the water with the eyes looking straight in front. Ask them to twist their head lightly to their most comfortable side, through an angle of 90 degrees. Tell them that when half of their face is clear of the water, they should aim to turn the mouth a little further so that they take in air.

Teaching points

- Encourage pupils to twist the mouth back towards the shoulder for protection.
- Get them to twist their head back towards the centre and blow out through their mouth.
- Ask pupils to try this with knees bent in the water. Again, the face should be lowered into the water.
- Suggest to the class that they experiment in order to discover their most comfortable breathing side.
- Encourage pupils to turn the head the right amount by getting them to 'bite an apple on their shoulder'.

The next phase is to get class members to decide which side is the best on which to breathe. If a pupil decides to breathe to the right, the pupil's head should turn every time the left hand enters the water and the face should be centralised prior to the right hand entering (and vice versa if the breathing happens to be to the left).

After experimenting while crouching in the water, the class should continue to experiment while swimming with the face in the water. One good way is to try breathing every four strokes. The biggest single problem among beginners is that they breathe in water by mistake, often due to beginning the breathing out phase at the wrong time. This comes about because the learner thinks that he or she is breathing out when the nose returns to the water.

The reality is that he or she is not breathing out early enough, and during this period the water enters the pupil's nose. The problem is compounded because the swimmer is already slightly confused over the change of pressure as the face moves through air pressure back to water pressure. The best way to overcome this is to get pupils to exhale before the nose and mouth have re-entered the water.

Backstroke

The backstroke leg action on its own should be practised thoroughly before moving on to introduce the arms. The legs are important as both propulsive and balancing agents. Strengthen the legs and introduce variety during lessons by getting pupils to try kicking with the body in slightly different positions in the water, so that they are working to get the body higher in the water. Each position will present a different challenge and can be brought about by moving the arms to different positions.

Start with pupils kicking with their arms by their side, i.e. with their palms face down in close proximity to the upper legs. Then ask them to lift both arms up so that the hands are held together above the head. This has the effect of lowering the hips and legs. A further alternative practice is to get pupils to try kicking with one hand above the head on the water, vertically in line with the forehead. They can also practise with the arms outstretched and thumbs linked. This lifts the hips but still makes the kick more difficult.

Following these four practices, you can start to introduce the arm movements. The general movement is with the arms swinging with the fingers stretched and the arms straight at the elbows. The hands circle backwards with the arms moving alternately. The movement is similar to that of the paddles in a rowing boat, except that the arms work alternately.

Teaching points

- Ask the class to stand on the pool side and simulate the arm movements on the side. Initially they should windmill the arms. This will help them to get the feeling of the backwards alternating movement.
- Encourage pupils to turn their hands to face outwards at the sides before swinging them backwards with the elbows and arms straight.
- When they have the feel of this movement, ask them to try it in the water.
- Pupils should aim to enter the little finger first as the hand turns outwards.
- The arms should be stretched out with the elbows straight.
- Teach pupils that the hands should enter the water between 1 and 2 o'clock on an imaginary clock, the centre of the head being at 12 o'clock.
- The next move should be for pupils to drive the fingers backwards until they are about 40cm (12 inches) under the water, then the hand is turned in line with the surface and cupped for the pull.

Some of the early problems are:

- Pupils splashing too much with their arms when entering their hands into the water. **Tip**: get them to lead with their little finger and hand turned out as the hand is lifted from the water at the hips during the recovery phase.
- Pupils have difficulty in fitting in the arms and getting them to time properly with the legs. **Tip**: you may want to break the stroke down initially so that they work with one arm only while keeping the other arm down by their side.
- Some pupils might over-kick, taking as many as eight kicks to each arm cycle. They need to be given time to develop the strength in the trunk muscles for the arm pull.
- The most important but often forgotten element of the stroke is the breathing. **Tip**: ask pupils to concentrate on pushing bad air out with the mouth. The breathing should be regular and continuous.

Breaststroke

Breaststroke leg action with a float is not an easy movement to learn. For many pupils, it is not particularly propulsive initially. Therefore, it is probably better to leave the introduction of the breaststroke legs until later in the learning process. This is a generality as not all pupils will have the same strengths and skills, and all will learn at different rates.

In breaststroke, the pull should be circular and wide but never straight back. As with backstroke, it is a good idea to give an impression of the movement by getting the class to go through the pulling movements on the pool side first. After a few initial attempts at the movement, ask pupils to pair up and get the partner's arms to act as resistance to help with the feel for the pull. They can do this by pressing hand to hand in the opposite direction during the first part of the pull when it is imitated in a standing position. Following this, the class can try the pull in the water with the legs trailing.

Slowly, as pupils become more comfortable with the pull, the leg kick can be added. Encourage pupils to feel the backward and downward drive of the feet. One way of teaching them is to take two arm pulls to one leg kick at first, or vice versa, until pupils feel balanced enough for one pull, one kick.

In progressive steps, the class should be channelled towards being able to pull and then kick afterwards. Slowly, the breathing should be introduced. The class should be encouraged to lower the face to the water's surface and to aim to blow the fingers away as the hands are projected forward and away from the face. The inhalation needs to take place when the hands have been pulled back and round until the hands are immediately in front of the chin.

Breaststroke legs

While breaststroke has the advantage of being a stroke which offers the option of swimming with the face out of the water, which may encourage the more timid pupils, it has the disadvantage of having complex leg movements. You will find that some pupils neither have the ankle strength nor the flexibility necessary to be able to make the movements. These pupils will often swim with the toes pointed rather than curled.

Here, again, start out of the water with pupils lying one by one over a bench or equivalent so that the legs hang down and are capable of being bent at the knees. Run through the general movement of the legs with the class. Then get pupils to enter the water and hold the rail or side of the pool, with their elbows against the wall. They can use their elbows to lever their feet up closer to the surface. Get pupils to start with their feet and legs straight out behind. The toes should be stretched out. First, instruct pupils to bend the knees and to lift the heels towards the surface. The effect is that the lower leg is lifted above the height of the upper leg. The knees should be turned slightly outwards so as to be approximately 40 degrees from the vertical.

Now ask pupils to bend the knees steadily. As the knees bend, the heels are squeezed up to the behind. When they have reached the behind, encourage pupils to rotate their ankles outwards at an angle of 45 degrees from the vertical. The soles of the feet face backwards away from the line of direction of the feet. They then push backwards. The knees now begin to straighten and the feet kick back and continue their outward rotation. During this rotation, the toes adopt a curled position. It is important to get pupils to keep their upper legs as still as possible, so as to prevent the knees being drawn up under the body. Teach that the heels are finally brought together in a whip-like manner. Pupils can do this by changing the emphasis at the toes by curling rather than pointing the toes.

Teaching points

- Watch out for pupils who bring their knees up too far under their body as this can increase resistance. **Tip**: get them to aim to lift their heels towards their behind.
- A good way of strengthening the legs by placing extra resistance on them is to increase from one to two, or even three, floats while kicking legs only.

PART 3
LESSON PLANS

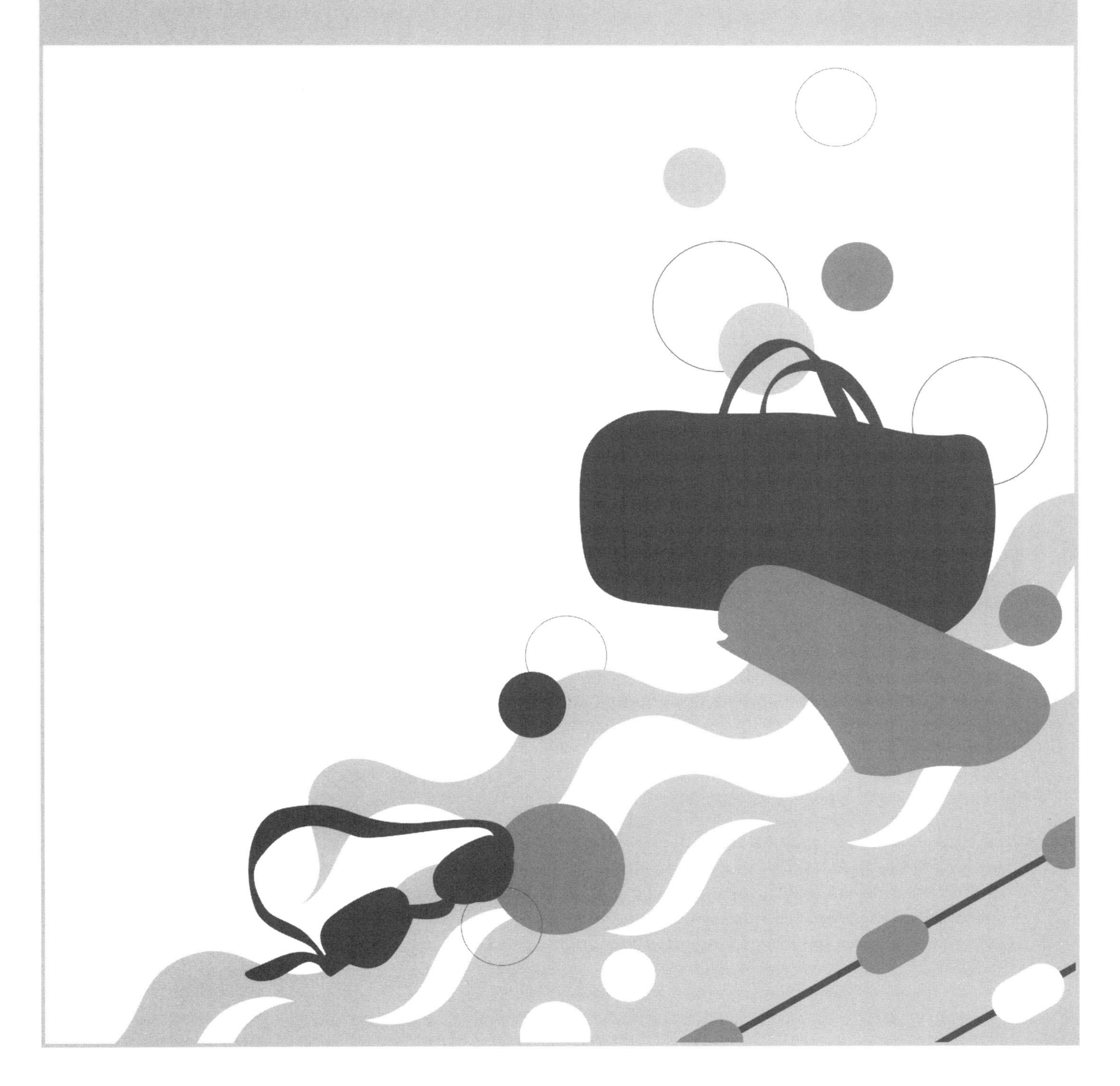

CHAPTER 14

LESSON PLANS

This chapter contains a scheme of lessons you may wish to employ with your class. In order to provide a framework, it assumes the following:

- that each swimming lesson lasts for 30 minutes
- that the class is split into two groups – one group of complete learners and one group of pupils with previous experience of swimming who can already swim 25 metres. While not foolproof, this structure is indicative of many school swimming situations where one group swims in the deep end and another in the shallow end of a pool.

Each lesson will contain the following:

- the lesson theme – what the lesson aims to provide and achieve
- introduction – water safety/good practice at the pool, questions and points (2 minutes)
- the skill/stroke practice and teaching tips
- legs, arms and/or body position
- contrasting activity/conclusion
- evaluating skill/stroke practice element of lesson.

There is an extremely useful Qualifications and Curriculum Authority (QCA) web site (www.nc.uk.net/safeswimming/teach/non-swimmers) that provides ideas for swimming lessons.

The QCA identifies three levels of swimming and, for the purpose of identifying the standards achieved by each pupil, it has three standards:

- *Non-swimmers* – pupils need to be able to: work confidently and safely in and around water; use basic actions to move around and across the pool using swimming aids and supports.

- *Beginners* – pupils need to be able to: remember, repeat and link actions effectively when moving on and below the surface of the water; swim short distances (5–15 metres) confidently with little or no support from others, and with few or no swimming aids.

- *Intermediate* – pupils need to be able to: swim with good body position and timing when using strokes and personal survival skills on their front and back; co-ordinate their arm and leg actions with breathing, showing quality and control for more than 45 seconds.

The QCA also provides strong guidance on how you can evaluate and improve the performance of pupils. This is as follows:

- *Non-swimmers.* Pupils need to be able to:
  - watch and copy what others have done
  - describe and explain their own and others' actions, skills and ideas
  - recognise actions that work better than others
  - recognise the need to follow safety rules in and around water.

- *Beginners*. Pupils need to be able to:
  - copy, repeat and describe actions accurately
  - compare their own actions with others
  - use information they gain to improve their own swimming
  - recognise and describe risks in and around water.

- *Intermediate*. Pupils need to be able to:
  - identify aspects of work that need improving and suggest how to practise to bring about this improvement
  - recognise when there is good co-ordination of arms, legs and breathing
  - improve their effectiveness and efficiency by making adjustments as they swim.

(Source: Qualifications and Curriculum Authority)

The following course is split into 12 lessons, for both a beginners and an intermediate group on a once-weekly basis. Each lesson is themed to include the activity in one column and teaching tips in another. Essentially, the course is designed for either Year 5 or Year 6. The first 12 lessons (pages 66–78) are for beginners; the next 12 (pages 79–92) for intermediate.

Beginners

Lesson Plan 1 • 30 minutes

Themes and objectives: Acquainting pupils with the water for the first time

Introduction	**Theme of introduction** Hygiene at the pool.	**Introductory points/questions** • Lay out the signals for when pupils should stop, look and listen. • Consideration for others in pool changing rooms. • Actions which should be taken after changing and before entering the water. • Actions to be taken on leaving the water.
Skill/stroke practice	**Teaching progression** Kicking legs while seated on pool side.	**Teaching tips** • Encourage pupils to make as much splash as possible. • Keep eyes fixed in front with hands resting firmly and with palms facing down on pool side.
	Entering the water individually for the first time.	• Get pupils to work in a safe depth, preferably in a corner of the pool. • Identify danger spots. • Adopt initial balanced position by curling toes over the side before commencing activity. • Keep head upright and eyes fixed in front as much as possible. • Feel for bottom with feet and bend knees.
Legs	**Teaching progression** Move freely around pool making different shapes with the arms and legs, stopping still when told to do so.	**Teaching tips** • Bend knees and crouch slightly. • Aim to stretch the arms as wide as possible when moving round the pool to maintain balance. • Start with small paces, letting the water take part of the weight of the body. • Pupils to describe what others are doing.
	Pupils make bouncing movement around pool.	Encourage pupils to bounce lightly from one foot to the other.
	Splashing legs while holding on to pool side.	Hands on wall, elbows against side so that legs can rise to the surface more easily when straightened.
Balance/ timing/ co-ordination	**Teaching progression** Push from bottom of pool while holding a woggle or float.	**Teaching tips** • Pupils need to stretch out. • More confident pupils can try with partner.
Contrasting activity	**Activity** Travelling game – split the class into smaller groups. Pupils link hands and travel in a circle round the pool.	**Teaching tips** Try moving in one direction and then the other.
	Get circle to continue to face in. While holding hands, alternate pupils lower themselves as far as possible into the water.	Aim to duck shoulders under water.
Evaluating lesson	**Main skill** Entering water.	**Points to watch out for** • Did all pupils manage this comfortably? • Were you able to correct those pupils that had difficulty? • Will all pupils be capable of affecting an entrance without assistance at next lesson?

Lesson Plan 2 • 30 minutes

Themes and objectives: Introducing breathing and building on initial confidence

Introduction	**Theme of introduction** Safety at the pool.	**Introductory points/questions** • How to move around the pool side when out of the water. • How to act when there are others around you in the water. • Being aware of depth and space around pupils. • Ask pupils if it is easier to get into shallow water or deep.
Skill/stroke practice	**Teaching progression** Repeat exercise on entry to pool.	**Teaching tips** Reiterate key points as above.
	Travel anywhere in pool.	• Concerned swimmers should be allowed to start while holding on to pool side. • Look behind before stepping backwards. • Ask pupils to hop instead of walking to encourage variety.
	While holding on to pool side, take both feet off the bottom.	Pupils should be encouraged to bend their knees to their chest.
	Blowing egg flips, table tennis balls.	• Start pupils crouching. • Progress to pupils placing nose on surface of water. • Encourage pupils to move and blow. • Less confident will start by pushing ball or egg flip with nose. Encourage to progress to blowing. • Ask pupils to find a partner and blow against partner.
	Blow out at pool rail.	• Recommend to pupils that they try practising with their face underwater in wash basins at home. • Pupils should practise blowing out before the face actually meets the water, to prevent water going up nose on initial contact.
	Blow out while facing and holding partner's hands.	One partner sinks and blows while the other stands, and vice versa.
	Blow out while opening eyes.	One pupil sinks face and counts the number of fingers their partner has opened under water.
Legs	**Teaching progression** Hold side of pool, kick hard and breathe out.	**Teaching tips** • Pupils are encouraged to breathe and kick while facing pool side. • Pupils then place their face in water and breathe out while kicking.
Contrasting activity	**Activity** Pupils move around pool on their feet, aiming to touch as many other pupils in the class as possible.	**Teaching tips** Ask pupils to count as many pupils tagged as possible.
	Pupils start in the middle of the learner's pool. While keeping their arms by their side, they walk as quickly as possible, aiming to touch all four sides of the pool.	Pupils are encouraged to move in a controlled way and to explore the most effective way of moving quickly and safely.
Evaluating lesson	**Main skill** Learning to breathe.	**Points to watch out for** • Can pupils apply breathing when kicking? • Can pupils balance air and water pressure when placing their face in water?

Lesson Plan 3 • 30 minutes

Beginners

Themes and objectives: Introduction of the alternate leg action

Introduction	**Theme of introduction** How swimming can benefit health.	**Introductory points/questions** • Explain the use of energy when swimming. • Discuss which forms of swimming will use up the most energy. • Outline to pupils the importance of good eating and exercise – balancing what one puts into the body with what one takes out. • Outline the benefit of swimming at times outside school hours
Skill/stroke practice	**Teaching progression** Pupils enter water and kick at rail/pool side.	**Teaching tips** • Pupils repeat previous practice by kicking at rail/pool side. • Encourage pupils to shake their feet while keeping the toes pointed.
Legs	**Teaching progression** • Pupils should explore ways of floating with arms wrapped around two floats and, later, one float. • Pupils kick while holding two floats. • Encourage pupils to try with single float.	**Teaching tips** • Pupils should be taught how to hold a float while standing in the water. • Pupils should try keeping their arms straight at the elbows and point their toes.
	Ask pupils to kick fast and slow and try kicking with the hips turned to the side.	Pupils should try kicking sideways, first with both arms above head holding float and then with one arm wrapped around float.
	Pupils try kicking while holding the float in different ways and then kicking with a different number of floats.	Encourage pupils to experiment with different positions so that they develop the kicking position most suited to them as individuals.
Contrasting activity	**Activity** Work with a partner for games.	**Teaching tips** • Copy what partner is doing. • Then mirror what partner is doing. • Move around pool, dodging to avoid partner.
Evaluating lesson	**Main skill** Mastering main kicking action for dog paddle and front crawl legs.	**Points to watch out for** • Have pupils been able to kick without either too much splash or without their feet being too low in the water? • Are pupils maintaining a balanced position with the hips close to the surface of the water?

Lesson Plan 4 • 30 minutes

Themes and objectives: Introduction of the arm movements for the first time when swimming; on this occasion, dog paddle

Introduction	**Theme of introduction** When pupils should swim and not swim.	**Introductory points/questions** • Explain to pupils what to watch out for. • Ask pupils when they think they shouldn't go swimming. • Explain when the class teacher should be consulted, e.g. open sores, ear infections, coughs, catarrh and diarrhoea.
Skill/stroke practice	**Teaching progression** Pupils are asked to stand in water and to explore different hand positions.	**Teaching tips** • Pupils should crouch in water so that the shoulders are level with the surface of the water. • Pupils should try to compose different hand movements with different hand surfaces. • Start with arms out straight; pupils sweep inside of the hand and arms towards imaginary line in front of the nose. • Pupils should then sweep back with outside of hand. • Pupils try to press down with palm and then back up. • Next, they should try making figure-of-eight movements in the water. • Encourage pupils to find the most effective shape for the hand movements. • Finally, encourage them to feel the effect of lifting the hand over the water's surface and pressing down.
Arms	**Teaching progression** Dog paddle movements with arms underwater while standing.	**Teaching tips** • Task pupils to make dog paddle movements while standing. • Shoulders should be down on the surface of the water. • Fingers should stretch out so that the arms straighten at the elbow • Encourage pupils to bend the elbows following the maximum extension and pull the hands back towards the stomach.
	Float with arms stretched in front and leg kick.	• Pupils are asked to lower shoulders to surface and push lightly off the bottom. • Arms should be stretched with the face above the water. • Instruct pupils to lightly kick their legs.
	Pupils co-ordinate arms with kick.	• Pupils follow above practice but start to pull with hands back to stomach. • Tell pupils to imagine that they are lying down and pulling themselves along a rope running through the centre of the stomach. • Encourage pupils to stay balanced by keeping their chin on the water. • Breathing out is also important and needs to continue.
Contrasting activity	**Activity** • Experimenting with different floating positions • Float sitting on a float. • Mushroom float with arms wrapped around shins (head above water). • Float with arms and legs straight while lying on front (head up).	**Teaching tips** • Explain to pupils the basics about floating, i.e. using the position of the head to alter the central position of buoyancy. • Experiment with different head positions to alter overall body position.
Evaluating lesson	**Main skill** Use of dog paddle arms.	Points to watch out for • At the end of the lesson, can pupils pull continuously or do they break their strokes? • Do they understand how to co-ordinate their arms and legs, and do they have a basic understanding of the timing? • At the end of the lesson, can pupils explain the fundamentals of the core dog paddle movement?

Lesson Plan 5 • 30 minutes

Themes and objectives: First stage of backstroke progression

Introduction	**Theme of introduction** Pupils may need to swim outdoors and not always indoors.	**Introductory points/questions** • Pupils need to understand the conditions outdoors are completely different: often colder; the water darker and less accessible. • In cold water, pupils should not move more than is necessary and should not move to keep warm. • If they fall in, they should hold on to support if possible and face away from waves.
Skill/stroke practice	**Teaching progression** Pupils float on their back aided by two floats.	**Teaching tips** • Pupils should start with shoulders on water and arms embracing a float each. • Task pupils to rest their ears on the water with eyes fixed on the pool roof. • Encourage pupils to point their toes in order to stretch legs.
	Pupils experiment with regaining standing position from back.	• Tuck up knees. • Bring chin forward and feel for bottom with feet.
	Pupils experiment with different head positions.	• Pupils try lifting the chin forward and then press the head back. • Encourage pupils to be balanced and in control of their own body. • Task them to find their best floating position.
	Pupils work with one float.	• Ask pupils to hold a float to their chest and to lightly push off the bottom of the pool. • They should let their feet float to the surface by pressing lightly on the back of their head. • As a variation, pupils can try a similar floating movement with the float behind the head.
Legs	**Teaching progression** Pupils sit over edge of pool and simulate the backstroke leg kick.	**Teaching tips** • Pupils should sit with their arms steadying them on the pool side. • They stretch their legs and kick continuously with an alternating upward movement of the big toe.
	Building on the floating exercise, the class now works with two floats each in the water.	• Pupils should stretch their arms out in line with their shoulders, each float wrapped under their arms. • Hint: pupils should try to kick an imaginary football off the surface towards the roof.
Balance/ timing/ co-ordination	**Teaching progression** When they are sufficiently confident, pupils can remove one and then both floats.	**Teaching tips** • Pupils should start with arms stretched out laterally in line with the shoulders. • When they have sufficient balance, the hands can be pulled in close to the hips.
Contrasting activity	**Activity** Obstacle course. Place a range of equipment in the water and get pupils to move over, under and around it. Hoops floating on the surface, woggles and rafts, can all be used.	**Teaching tips** Encourage as many pupils as possible to submerge through the hoops, even if it means pupils holding their nose in the first instance.
Evaluating lesson	**Main skill** Backstroke legs.	**Points to watch out for** • Are all pupils achieving an alternating action with their legs? • Are they adopting a poised body position in the water, i.e. are the hips and feet sufficiently close to the surface? • Is the leg action contributing sufficiently to this position and has the lesson helped them to achieve this?

Lesson Plan 6 • 30 minutes

Beginners

Themes and objectives: Transferring pupils to deeper water

Introduction	**Theme of introduction** Reinforce classroom water safety education by reiterating the Water Safety Code.	**Introductory points/questions** Main points: • spot the danger (how to do it) • take safety advice (outline) • go with a friend • learn how to help.
Skill/stroke practice	**Teaching progression** Practice getting into the water.	**Teaching tips** If pupils have only entered in the corner of the pool, try from the pool side away from the corner.
Arms	**Teaching progression** Pupils work on getting out of the pool. Start in shallow water.	**Teaching tips** • Pupils need to place their hands on the pool side and push lightly from the bottom with their feet. • The arms bend and then straighten as the legs push from the bottom of the pool.
	The class jumps into shallow water.	• Keep close to pool side. • Bend at the knees; keep the eyes firmly fixed in front. • Pupils take one pace forward into the water. • They should form a parachute shape with the arms to distribute the body weight across the surface. • The class should try this jump and the pulling out motion several times.
	Transfer this entrance and exit into deeper water.	• This may be a case of transferring the activity from a learner's pool to the shallow end of the main pool. • On jumping into deep water, pupils should bend their knees and start from a crouched position closer to the water.
Legs	**Teaching progression** Returning to shallow water, pupils once again lift both feet off the bottom.	**Teaching tips** • Aim to lift both knees to the chest. • Encourage pupils to try making running and then cycling movements in mid-water. • With the feet off the bottom, pupils make figure-of-eight movements with their hands.
	Transfer treading water to deeper water.	• Make gradual entry without jumping in. • Try to keep pupils as calm as possible. • Let small groups try this one at a time while the others sit on the pool deck. • Start with pupils close to the pool side. • Tell them to make slow, steady and regular movements. • Pupils should rest their chin on the surface and position their hands wide of the hips.
Contrasting activity	**Activity** Floating pond.	**Teaching tips** (See activity described on page 53.)
Evaluating lesson	**Main skill** Jumping into and treading water in deeper water.	**Points to watch out for** • The target should be for each pupil to manage treading in deep water for 10 seconds. • Have pupils used co-ordinated leg actions in treading water? • Has the lesson led to pupils being able to transfer the jumping, getting out and treading water skills learnt in the learner's pool/ shallow water to deeper water?

Lesson Plan 7 • 30 minutes

Themes and objectives: Building confidence in deeper water – drown-proofing, treading water and floating

Beginners

Introduction	**Theme of introduction** Understanding basic rescues, again reinforcing water safety work in the classroom.	**Introductory points/questions** Although pupils will not be strong enough swimmers yet, stress the importance of understanding the main ingredients of being involved with a basic rescue: • attracting the attention of the casualty • determining whether immediate support is available • keeping calm • making hand signals to help in assisting casualty to side.
Skill/stroke practice	**Teaching progression** Kicking front-crawl legs with float to warm up.	**Teaching tips** • Concentrate on 'long legs' – stretching the legs by pointing the toes and driving strongly towards the bottom on the down kick. • Work with a single float with the thumbs on top and each side of the float held. • Ask pupils to work in shallow water for this exercise.
	Swim dog paddle.	• Emphasise a flat body position. • The elbows should not be too far out at the sides during the pull. • Keep the head still.
Balance/ timing/ co-ordination	**Teaching progression** Mushroom float without and with face in water.	**Teaching tips** • Pupils should initially lift their knees to their chest and wrap their arms around their shins. • Follow by taking a breath and lowering their face in the water.
	Float freely in a range of ways.	• Encourage pupils to try floating freely and to experiment with the ways they can float both with the head up and the face in water. • Get them to describe what they are doing. • Ask pupils how they think they can improve on their float.
	Star-shaped float on back.	Encourage pupils to alter the position of their head and to explore how this can alter their overall body position.
	Star-shaped float on front.	• Again, ask pupils to explore how they can raise the position of the legs in the water. • Encourage them to tell you how they can achieve this.
	Pencil float rolling from front to back and vice versa.	• Pupils need to take a breath as their face may be underwater for a few seconds. • Ask the class to determine which part of the body will make them roll over. • Pupils should then select their most effective way of floating and practise this.
	Pupils start in deeper water by treading water followed by various forms of float.	All the above floats should be attempted in deeper water.
	Describe how pupils can hang in the water with the legs almost vertical (drown-proofing).	• Pupils should try 'hanging' with their arms in line with their shoulders. • Encourage them to press down with their hands to lift their heads and take a breath.

Lesson Plan 7 cont.

Contrasting activity	**Activity** Return to shallow water and then play sharks.	**Teaching tips** • One person is the tagged 'shark' and the rest of the class move freely round the pool. • The teacher shouts 'sharks' and the tagged person attempts to tag others. • When one or further pupils have been tagged, they join in as 'sharks'.
Evaluating lesson	**Main skill** Further confidence in deeper water.	**Points to watch out for** • Can pupils accurately transfer skills from shallow water? • Has each pupil managed to increase their capacity to tread water to between 10 and 20 seconds? • Can pupils confidently float in deeper water with the face under?

Lesson Plan 8 • 30 minutes

Beginners

Themes and objectives: Introducing the arms in backstroke

Introduction	**Theme of introduction** Building on previous lesson in explaining basic rescues – how pupils would help in a reach rescue.	**Introductory points/questions** • Explain the used of a rigid aid if subject is near the water's edge: reaching for the subject but lying flat on the ground and remaining firmly balanced. • Use non-rigid aid only as a second option. • Seize the subject by the wrist if there are no alternatives.
Skill/stroke practice	**Teaching progression** Backstroke legs without floats or with a single float for support.	**Teaching tips** • Pupils should concentrate on keeping the knees down under the surface. • Rehearse key points on regaining standing position in shallow water.
Arms	**Teaching progression** Pupils simulate arm movements while on pool side.	**Teaching tips** • Task pupils to windmill arms. • Run through position on clock where hand should enter by demonstrating with one pupil lying flat on the ground or on a raised area. • Explain the importance of keeping the head still and overall control of the arms.
	Pupils re-enter the water and start with backstroke legs. They slowly introduce a single arm movement.	• Suggest pupils bring one arm back once in every six kicks initially. • They should lead with the little finger and turn the palm outwards. • The hands should not interfere with the head on entry. The head should rest on the same plain throughout. • Get pupils to press the head back by focusing the eyes on the pool roof so that the legs and hips are not too low in the water.
Balance/ timing/ co-ordination	**Teaching progression** Pupils slowly increase number of arm entries per leg kicks.	**Teaching tips** When pupils can manage the arm action on their chosen arm, encourage them to work with alternating arms.
	Breathing is now introduced.	• Stress that breathing is extremely important on backstroke but is often forgotten. • Ask pupils to concentrate on pushing bad air out. • Work with arms and legs to achieve this.
Contrasting activity	Simon says.	The teacher starts by leading the tasks but later a pupil leads the tasks.
Evaluating lesson	**Main skill** Backstroke arms.	**Points to watch out for** • This lesson should result in pupils being able to lift at least one arm over the water. • Can pupils achieve the arm skills while maintaining a good flat position on the surface?

Lesson Plan 9 • 30 minutes

Themes and objectives: Establish key principles of push off and glide

Beginners

Introduction	**Theme of introduction** Continuing theme with rescues: throwing rescues.	**Introductory points/questions** • Ask pupils when they would use a throwing rescue. • Run through what sort of aids could be used for such a rescue. • Pupils should then determine how effective a throwing rescue would be compared to a reach rescue.
Skill/stroke practice	**Teaching progression** Pupils warm up by kicking on their front with a float.	**Teaching tips** Work on pressing shoulders down in the water and leaning lightly towards the float in order to lift the legs.
	Dog paddle with concentration on pressing the hands back to the hips.	Encourage pupils to concentrate on the length and range of their pull and to work on maximising this range.
	Dog paddle with stroke counting.	• Pupils should count the number of strokes it takes to get from one side to the other. • Ask them how they feel they could improve their stroke efficiency and decrease the number of strokes taken.
Legs	**Teaching progression** Pupils start glide by pushing off the bottom.	**Teaching tips** • Stress the importance of the glide as a tool for streamlining the body and reducing the time taken between two points. • Pupils should push from bottom with arms outstretched and the inside of the arms around the ears.
	Practise the start position for gliding from the wall.	• Run through the key elements of the start position. • After holding the pool side behind, what are the next moves? Explain.
	Practise the push itself.	• Outline the target body position. • Work on lengthening the push on each attempt. • Explain when the legs and then the arms should be introduced using dog paddle as an example.
Balance/ timing/ co-ordination	Practise the push off with the introduction of the arms and legs.	
Evaluating lesson	**Main skill** Push off and glide.	**Points to watch out for** • Determine the level of success based on the percentage of the class that can push and glide with their face in the water and regain a standing position in the water. • All pupils should aim to push off by drawing their arms up by the sides of their body rather than throwing their hands over the water.

Lesson Plan 10 • 30 minutes

Beginners

Themes and objectives: Revision session on backstroke and dog paddle skills

Introduction	**Theme of introduction** Emphasis on courtesy for other users.	**Introductory points/questions** • Outline that most pool use is shared. • Noise and behaviour in changing rooms. • Impression made on entering and leaving pool. • Taking all personal equipment on leaving.
Skill/stroke practice	**Teaching progression** Dog paddle working on full stroke practice.	**Teaching tips** • Blow out into water. • Feel the pressure of the water on the hand and wrist as the pull takes place. • Head to be kept still except when breathing out.
	Dog paddle races across widths.	Introduce some dog paddle team races between teams of four pupils; pupils to start in water.
	Revise push and glide followed by dog paddle.	Pupils do this individually.
	Backstroke legs trying different position for arms.	• Task pupils to swim with hands by sides. • Increase difficulty by asking them to hold hands above their head in the air and then by placing one and/or two hands on the surface above the head.
	Backstroke.	Ask pupils to imagine they are balancing a cup of tea on their forehead.
Contrasting activity	**Activity** Sculling.	• Pupils float on their back with their hands by their sides. • Working from the elbows, encourage the class to make small figure-of-eight movements. • Fingers should start in line with arm, the hand tilted sideways and the palm swept outwards and then back in. • The aim is to propel the body forwards on the back. • Keep a streamlined shape with the head in a line. • Pupils should point their toes and keep the legs together and straight.
Evaluating lesson	**Main skill** Reinforcement and revision lesson.	**Points to watch out for** • This lesson seeks to ensure that pupils are kicking rhythmically in both strokes. • Check to ensure that the arm movements on front and back are propulsive and do not waste energy. • Determine whether pupils are splashing too much in making the strokes.

Lesson Plan 11 • 30 minutes

Themes and objectives: Introduction of front crawl arms

Introduction	**Theme of introduction** The right equipment for swimming.	**Introductory points/questions** Set out guidelines on swimming caps, tying the hair back, approaches to jewellery and 'long legged' costumes worn by boys.
Skill/stroke practice	**Teaching progression** Push and glide.	**Teaching tips** • Revise push and glide technique. • Pupils should then add the leg kick and return to standing position.
Arms	**Teaching progression** Rehearse arm movement on pool side.	**Teaching tips** • Run through arm movements on pool side. • Ask pupils to bend forward at the hips and assimilate the arm movements with the head to the front. • Pupils should be encouraged to bend their elbows and recover their arms forward with their thumbs close to their body.
	Front crawl in water with head to the front.	• Pupils start with the push off glide. • They should introduce the legs and then, with the head to the front, add the arms. • At this stage, there should be no emphasis on the breathing timing. • Pupils should aim to slide the fingers in through the surface rather than to slap the hands.
Balance/ timing/ co-ordination	**Teaching progression** Front crawl with breathing.	• Introduce the breathing standing in the water. • Progress to the prone position. • Encourage pupils to breathe towards one shoulder. • The signal for this is when one hand enters the water at the front. • Pupils should breathe towards the shoulder where they feel most comfortable. • Get pupils to feedback their experience. • Try not to lift the head on taking a breath.
Contrasting activity	**Activity** Touching the bottom of the pool with different parts of the body.	Variations include the hands, bottom and knees.
Evaluating lesson	**Main skill** Front crawl arms.	**Points to watch out for** • Assess at the end of the lesson whether pupils remain streamlined. • Can they time the breathing so as to take a breath when breathing to the side and blow out when the face returns to the front?

Lesson Plan 12 • 30 minutes

Beginners

Themes and objectives: Pupils become familiar with moving underwater

Introduction	**Theme of introduction** Good habits when swimming.	**Introductory points/questions** Introduce the following ideas: • using the toilet before swimming • not wearing dirty shoes in the pool changing rooms and side • not eating for more than an hour before swimming.
Skill/stroke practice	**Teaching progression** Start and warm up by continuing the front crawl practice.	**Teaching tips** Suggest pupils 'bite an apple' off their shoulder to give them a feel for the breathing movement.
	Move on to underwater practices: duck down and reach for bottom.	• Pupils should be encouraged to touch the bottom with any sensible part of the body. • Ask them to open their eyes and find out how many other pupils they can see under the water.
	Under and over hoops.	• Place hoops on the surface of the water. • Pupils should link thumbs in front, duck through hoops and come up under others. • Pupils should try to keep the inside of the arms around the ears, mimicking the position of an actual dive.
	Surface dive.	• Pupils should start with breaststroke-like movement. • Ask them to pull down and immediately drop their chin to their chest. • Tip: the hips will now be parallel with the surface of the water. Ask pupils to point their toes so that the body follows in one straight line.
	Surface dive to collect brick or equivalent, lighter object.	• Pupils should continue to work in shallow water/learner's pool. • Encourage class to open its eyes and look for an object on the bottom. • Whole activity needs to be seen as a build up to introducing diving.
Contrasting activity	**Activity** Team relays swimming with ball.	**Teaching tips** Pupils should swim dog paddle or front crawl with head up. The ball is pushed in front of team member.
Evaluating lesson	**Main skill** Swimming under water.	**Points to watch out for** The key factor with this lesson is to make sure that all pupils are acquainted with these basic skills as the forerunner of diving instruction to come.

Lesson Plan 1 • 30 minutes

Themes and objectives: Introducing front crawl arms

Introduction	**Theme of introduction** Avoiding accidents at the pool.	**Introductory points/ questions** Pupils should be alerted to a series of problems that might arise from their actions towards others; for example: • pushing on pool side • pushing others when at pool edge • running on side • splashing.
Skill/stroke practice	**Teaching progression** Recap on the push and glide as a forerunner for front crawl.	**Teaching tips** • Start with both hands simultaneously from the wall. • Release the hands and bend the elbows in order to bring them under the body. • When the hands reach the front of the face, push with the feet on the wall and straighten arms at the elbows.
Legs	**Teaching progression** Work on introducing the alternating leg kick. Start by pushing off the bottom with the arms stretched out in front and then move to pushing from the wall.	**Teaching tips** • Concentrate on rhythmic, steady kick. • Stress kick to keep the body as streamlined and as close to the surface as possible.
	Introduce the arm movements without stressing the breathing at this stage. Concentrate on giving pupils a feel for the directional pattern of the arms.	• Pupils should aim to kick with their face in the water and to recover their arms over the water at their hips. • Keep the thumbs close to the body as the elbows are bent and the hands brought forward. • Tell pupils to stretch with their fingers and to straighten their arms at the elbows. • The stretch out can be slow and contain a pause.
	• Keep pupils moving across the widths, preferably from a push and glide each time. • In this exercise, start to emphasis the pull.	• Pupils should aim for a controlled hand entry and slide the fingers into the water without too much splash. • Do not hurry the arms. • As soon as the fingers and palms can feel the water, press back towards the stomach. • When the hand has reached the stomach, push past the hips.
Balance/ timing/ co-ordination	**Teaching progression** Outline the timing and co-ordination of the arms in relation to the legs. Some pupils will have already started doing this, but for others it will need re-emphasising.	**Teaching tips** • Pupils should enter with one arm as the other arm is being lifted from the water at the hips. • At this stage, any number of leg kicks to each arm cycle is acceptable. You can suggest six beats to an arm cycle at a much later stage in pupils' swimming development. • They should aim to keep the forehead on the surface of the water. • Ask pupils to check where their hands are positioned by being conscious of where the trailing hand is as the other hand enters the water.
Contrasting activity	**Activity** Standing and walking water polo.	**Teaching tips** The whole class can take part. • Establish two markers at each side of the learners' pool for goals. • Avoid introducing too many rules. • Let the game flow as much as possible.
Evaluating lesson	**Main skill** Co-ordinating the front crawl arms and legs.	**Points to watch out for** • Can pupils enter the hands smoothly? • Do they pull with the hands down the centre line of the body towards the stomach?

Intermediate

Lesson Plan 2 • 30 minutes

Themes and objectives: Co-ordinating the front crawl breathing with the arms

Introduction	**Theme of introduction** Actions to be taken if a pupil sees another swimmer in difficulty at the pool.	**Introductory points/questions** • Assess how the pupil can help. • Determine whether other adults are in a position to help. • Drawing the attention of the lifeguard.
Skill/stroke practice	**Teaching progression** Pupils warm up by using a float for front crawl legs and back crawl legs across widths.	**Teaching tips** • On back-crawl legs, aim to keep knees under the surface. • Point and stretch toes on up-kick. • On front crawl legs, work on keeping the feet close together and making the kick as vertical as possible. Avoid breathing to the side and kicking too laterally.
Arms	**Teaching progression** Start by running through the front crawl breathing on the pool side.	**Teaching tips** • Pupils should decide which side they feel it would be most comfortable to breathe on. • Run through the timing of the inhalation in relation to the arm cycle.
	Pupils return to the water. They first revise the front crawl movements, concentrating on the arm and leg movements.	Concentrate on making all the movements feel easy and unhurried.
	The breathing is now added.	• Pupils breathe in when one hand enters the water. • If they breathe towards the right shoulder, the signal for this should be when the left hand enters the water. • Explain that pupils should take air in through the mouth and start to blow out just before the nose and mouth re-enter the water.
	Revise the front crawl movement with the full breathing.	• Pupils should watch others and compare what they are doing. • Encourage pupils to pause and take their time when breathing in. • When they blow out, ask them to relax and to concentrate on keeping their eyes fixed on the bottom of the pool about three feet in front of them.
	Build the practice in short five-metre swims.	Get pupils to describe what they did and explain how they think they could improve. Remind them to: • blow out smoothly • not to hurry the movements • try to pull the water more strongly by feeling the water with the hands and making the pull longer. Get pupils to start to breathe every stroke, i.e. once in every arm cycle.
Contrasting activity	**Activity** Spinning tub.	**Teaching tips** • Pupils float and 'sit in' water with their head on the surface and their knees drawn up to the chest. • They should invent ways of rotating the body using the hands while keeping the knees up. • Try moving round one way and then the other. • Describe figure-of-eight hand movements to facilitate action.
Evaluating lesson	**Main skill** Introduction of front crawl breathing.	**Points to watch out for** • Evaluate whether pupils can breathe comfortably. • Determine whether they can breathe without the legs dropping too far and the movement becoming unstreamlined. • Do pupils turn their head to the side only or lift their head to breathe in?

Intermediate

Lesson Plan 3 • 30 minutes

Themes and objectives: Introduce the breaststroke arms

Introduction	**Theme of introduction** The dangers of swimming alone.	**Introductory points/questions** • Never swim alone. • Why pupils should not swim alone. • Who they understand to be a suitable supervisor.
Skill/stroke practice	**Teaching progression** Warm up with some easy dog paddle from one side to the other.	**Teaching tips** • Pupils should concentrate on length of stroke without pulling the elbows too far behind shoulders. • Follow up with one or two quick-fire races across the pool.
Arms	**Teaching progression** Start the breaststroke by getting a pupil who can already swim it to demonstrate the stroke or by watching another pool user perform the stroke.	**Teaching tips** • Explain to pupils the timing of the stroke – pull, breathe, kick and stretch out. • Outline that breaststroke is a jointed stroke with the knees, ankles, elbows and shoulders all playing a part. • Relate similarity to that of a frog.
	Pupils push off from the wall and make round, circular movements.	• Keep the hands under the water – at least, initially. • The hands make a small movement. • Keep the hands in front of the face. • The hands scull out and scull in.
	Pupils work in pairs, each partner practising in turns.	• Pupils explain to their partner where they think he/she is going wrong. • Encourage pupils to start stretching out and straightening their arms at the elbows during the recovery.
Balance/ timing/ co-ordination	**Teaching progression** Add the breathing – encourage pupils to lift their head to breathe in at the end of the pull, when the hands have circled in front of the head.	**Teaching tips** Pupils should lower their face and breathe out with their arms straight together at the elbows in front of them.
Contrasting activity	**Activity** Pupils lay out flat on their back with their eyes looking up towards the pool roof.	**Teaching tips** • Instruct pupils to make sculling movements with palms open towards their feet. • Ask them to experiment by travelling feet-first in the opposite direction. This can be facilitated by making small breaststroke-like pulls while lying on their back.
Evaluating lesson	**Main skill** Breaststroke arms.	**Points to watch out for** • Determine whether pupils have been able to make balanced and propulsive breaststroke arm movements even with the legs trailing. • Can pupils make small, compact movements that keep the elbows in front of the shoulders, or are the arm pulls too wide?

Lesson Plan 4 • 30 minutes

Themes and objectives: Adding the breaststroke legs to complete the stroke

Introduction	**Theme of introduction** Being outdoors on a boat.	**Introductory points/questions** • What to watch out for. • What equipment should be worn, e.g. life jacket. • Where to sit on a boat.
Skill/stroke practice	**Teaching progression** Pupils warm up by revising their backstroke full-stroke movements.	**Teaching tips** • Pupils should aim for a clean recovery over the water. • Imitate a rowing boat but with the arms being pulled higher than the oars over the water. • Aim to keep the head still with the water lapping round the ears.
Arms	**Teaching progression** Practise the arm movements from the previous session.	**Teaching tips** • Tell pupils to keep the movements circular. • Palms face out as the hands split to pull out. • Palms face in as the hands start to pull back in towards the face.
Legs	**Teaching progression** Demonstrate the leg action on the pool side using a pupil, preferably with the pupil draped over a raised surface.	**Teaching tips** • Stress the importance of lifting the heels towards the backside while not drawing the knees under the body. • Explain that the arms move first; a breath is then taken and the legs move afterwards.
	Pupils return to the water and work in pairs. One partner stands and slowly walks back while supporting the swimming pupil under the armpits (light support only).	• Pupils kick with flat feet, following the circular movements demonstrated on the pool side. • The heels are snapped together at the end of the movement.
	Pupils try the movement on their own, pulling or slightly resting on the arms as they part and close their legs slowly in front of them under the water.	• Explain that these early movements will be difficult. • Pupils should aim to drive with the soles of their feet in a whipping motion.
Balance/ timing/ co-ordination	**Teaching progression** The whole movement is now practised with a pause or a small glide at the finish of the kick.	**Teaching tips** • Good, streamlined position required. Pupils should try to ensure that their body is in a straight line with the arms and legs together stretched out at the end of each kick. Use the pause–glide to emphasise this. • Good, streamlined position required. Pupils should try to ensure that their body is in a straight line with the arms and legs together stretched out at the end of each kick. Use the pause–glide to emphasise this. • Ask them to quickly count '1–2' at the end of the arm recovery.
Contrasting activity	**Activity** Moving and floating.	**Teaching tips** • Pupils move around the pool using two moving and two floating actions until the whistle sounds. • Ask pupils to put up their hands and show unusual ways of floating and moving. • The whole class practises again, utilising some of the more unusual methods demonstrated.
Evaluating lesson	**Main skill** Co-ordinating the full-stroke breaststroke with the introduction of the legs.	**Points to watch out for** • Ask yourself: have pupils managed to make initial, frog-like movements (do not expect too much at first!)? • Can they kick back with their toes curled or do they kick with pointed toes? • Do they allow their feet to rise above the surface when they kick back?

Intermediate

Lesson Plan 5 • 30 minutes

Themes and objectives: Making the first dolphin-like movements

Introduction	**Theme of introduction** Explanation of why people should exercise.	**Introductory points/questions** • Outline why swimming is good exercise (stamina, flexibility, strength). • Explain the need to warm up before commencing exercise. • How much exercise should pupils take each week? • Get pupils to give examples of exercise they take each week. • Do any pupils swim regularly outside of school lessons?
Skill/stroke practice	**Teaching progression** Use the warm up to recap on the main elements of breaststroke. Pupils can work across the widths taking 10–20 seconds' rest between each width.	**Teaching tips** • Re-emphasise the timing of the stroke. • Look for good examples and ask the class to watch so that you can reiterate the main points.
Legs	**Teaching progression** Pupils should first float in the water with their face down. Then get them to rock gently up and down in a dolphin-like movement.	**Teaching tips** • Movements start from the shoulders. • The hips should follow the shoulders so that when the hips are down the shoulders are up and vice versa. • At first, emphasise the shoulders and hips rather than the legs.
	Pupils now try sinking underwater and feeling the resistance of the water around their body as they move.	• Keep the feet together and this time concentrate more on kicking with the feet. • Don't over-emphasise the up and down movement of the bottom and hips; this needs to be powerful and firm. • Shake the ankles and keep the toes long. • Ask pupils to see how far they can go on one breath.
	Move on to practise the dolphin-like movement with the hips turned sideways.	This can be tried as different variations: • on the surface with the hands by the sides • underwater • with the head resting on one arm out in front.
Contrasting activity	**Activity** Continuous floating.	**Teaching tips** • Pupils should be encouraged to float for as long as possible while expressing themselves with different floating shapes, e.g. star, mushroom, front, back, side, rolling as a log, etc. • Let them try a second time and hold a small competition to see who can hold their float for the longest while continuously changing the style of their float.
Evaluating lesson	**Main skill** Introducing dolphin kick and butterfly.	**Points to watch out for** • Evaluate whether the kick is strong yet not too broad. • Determine whether pupils can both make the movement and propel themselves for a distance of at least three metres.

Intermediate

Lesson Plan 6 • 30 minutes

Themes and objectives: Introduction of diving

Introduction	**Theme of introduction** The effect of swimming outdoors.	**Introductory points/questions** Explain the difference between swimming in a pool and swimming outdoors: • changes in temperature • tidal conditions • darkness of water and difficulty of being seen underwater.
Skill/stroke practice	**Teaching progression** Use the float to revise all four of the kicks: butterfly, backstroke, breaststroke and front crawl.	**Teaching tips** Once pupils have tried all four kicks with a float, allow them to kick without a float, either with their arms by their sides or with their arms out in front.
Balance/ timing/ co-ordination	**Teaching progression** Work with pupils on confidence-building measures: starting with controlled feet-first entries and a simple stepping-off the pool side.	**Teaching tips** • Keep the eyes focused in front and the back straight. • Stress the importance of ensuring that there is no one underwater or on the surface of the water before take off.
	Progress to jumping.	• Pupils should bend the knees before take off and keep the toes pointed on entry. • Later, pupils can enter with their toes pointed and their arms above their head.
	Pupils can now try entering the water in a star shape.	Again, get pupils to point their toes and keep their eyes directly in front.
	The more confident pupils can attempt a tuck jump.	Ask pupils to bend the knees to the chest and then point the toes to straighten the legs again on entry.
Contrasting activity	**Activity** • Surface diving for the less confident pupils. • For the very confident, build towards head-first entries with confidence activities, i.e. reaching down to the bottom of the pool and attempting a handstand.	**Teaching tips** When attempting a handstand: • pupils should stand on the bottom in shallow water • drop the chin and look towards the bottom of the pool • reach for the bottom with the finger tips • if the water takes the pupil past the vertical handstand, release the hands and curl up in a ball.
	• Push and glide for less confident pupils, directing their fingers towards the bottom of the pool. • More confident pupils swim breaststroke and pull down to go round in a somersault.	When attempting a somersault, pupils should tuck the chin on the chest, roll up in a ball and make one, big two-handed pull with the hands pressing down while in line with the shoulders.
Evaluating lesson	**Main skill** Ensuring that pupils are fully conversant with all feet-first entries in the water from the pool side.	**Points to watch out for** • Pupils should enter the water with the back straight. • Evaluate whether all pupils can execute each activity with full control.

Intermediate

Lesson Plan 7 • 30 minutes

Themes and objectives: More advanced diving

Introduction	**Theme of introduction** How to approach swimming when at the seaside.	**Introductory points/questions** • Swim between the flags. • Swim in line with the beach and not directly out. • Do not swim when the flags indicate otherwise. • Make sure that pupils are aware of the position of the lifeguard before swimming.
Skill/stroke practice	**Teaching progression** Warm up with stroke counting on front crawl and dog paddle.	**Teaching tips** • Pupils swim one width, counting the number of strokes it takes. • They repeat the exercise but concentrate on longer strokes by stretching out in front at the end of the recovery and pushing right through with their hands as close to the thighs as possible.
Balance/ timing/ co-ordination	**Teaching progression** Dives – starting with the most basic dive and then each dive becoming more challenging.	**Teaching tips** Key areas to stress with each of the dives: • preparation to take off • flight • entry • returning to the surface from underwater.
	Sitting dive.	• Pupils should have their legs wrapped over the edge, with feet placed on top of the swim rail. • Both arms are placed around the ears with the hands together in front of the head. • Pupils push with their feet from the pool side and direct their fingers towards the water. • Tell pupils to make a hole for their head with their hands – hands first followed by the rest of the body.
	Kneeling dive.	• Use a demonstration if there is a pupil who can already perform this dive. • Explain that the movement is similar to that of the sitting dive. • Legs should be straightened and pupils should aim to get their hips as high as possible. • After entering the water, the hands should be turned back up towards the surface.
	Crouch dive.	• Once again, stress the need for a controlled movement. • Pupils can crouch low and close to the water at first and then slowly move to a more upright starting position.
	Standing dive.	• Those pupils that have managed the other dives with a level of competence can now attempt the full standing dive. • The movements are much the same as for the crouch dive but the starting position is higher on the pool side.
Contrasting activity	**Activity** Over-and-under relay with a ball.	**Teaching tips** • Split the class into teams. • The teams stand in a line across the pool, every other pupil with his or her feet astride. • A ball is passed backwards from pupil to pupil with the ball alternatively passed over the head and between the legs. • The pupil at the end of the line then swims with the ball to the front and the sequence starts again.

Intermediate

Lesson Plan 7 cont.

	Twisting relay.	• The formation is exactly the same but pupils line up back-to-back. • Pupils twist and pass the ball sideways, rugby fashion, to the next pupil. • The relay follows the pattern of the over-and-under relay.
Evaluating lesson	**Main skill** Learning basic diving.	**Points to watch out for** • Determine whether each pupil can bend the knees and enter the water with their hands first, i.e. without performing a belly flop. • Is the entry smooth and without too much splash?

Intermediate

Lesson Plan 8 • 30 minutes

Themes and objectives: Getting a feel for butterfly – an introduction to the stroke

Introduction	**Theme of introduction** The balance of eating and swimming.	**Introductory points/questions** • Importance of having a good breakfast before swimming. • Avoid swimming within an hour of eating. • Make sure you have something to eat within an hour after swimming. • Principle of what you take out through exercise, you need to put in through healthy food.
Skill/stroke practice	**Teaching progression** Start with backstroke legs across pool width.	**Teaching tips** Try placing the body in different positions: • hands by sides • hands out level with shoulders • hands over the head in line with the face • one arm outstretched on the surface of the water • both arms outstretched behind the head. Experiment with the different arm positions and feel their impact on the position of the legs and, in particular, the position of the hips.
Legs	**Teaching progression** Revise the basic dolphin leg movements.	**Teaching tips** • Pupils should try this by standing at the pool side, sinking the hips so that the push off takes place from lower down the wall. The movement can then be made with the arms out in front under the water. • Make small controlled movements – the stomach and hips only need to move lightly. • Keep the head and shoulders steady.
Arms	**Teaching progression** Introduce the arms by getting pupils to crouch down to the water's surface.	**Teaching tips** • Pupils lightly push off the bottom and throw their arms forward simultaneously over the water. • Aim to sink the face in the water before the hands meet the water. • The arms should be swept forward close to the surface and the hands enter in line with the shoulders.
	Pupils should now push off the bottom, throw their arms forward and try to make one or more dolphin kicks.	Encourage pupils to also try the reverse by making three or four kicks and then bringing their arms over the water.
	Encourage further basic movements by getting pupils to throw their arms over the water and then pause with their arms under the water stretched out in front.	Kick with the arms out in front and recover the arms afterwards.
Balance/ timing/ co-ordination	**Teaching progression** Try to give a correct feel for the breathing by getting pupils to practise lifting their head to take a breath in each arm cycle.	**Teaching tips** Explain the 'two heads rule' – lift the head up before the hands come out at the end of the pull and drop the head back in before the hands go in to make the pull.

Intermediate

Lesson Plan 8 cont.

Contrasting activity	**Activity** Pupils test their kicking power.	**Teaching tips** • Pupils line up halfway across the pool, facing one another in pairs with each pupil holding one end of a float. • Blow a whistle and ask them to keep their elbows straight and their arms out, and to kick against one another using front crawl legs. • The aim is to push your partner backwards using the power of the kick. • Change pairs and repeat.
Evaluating lesson	**Main skill** Very early stages of butterfly.	**Points to watch out for** • Do not expect too much in this evaluation. • Can all pupils throw their arms forward over the water? • Can all pupils attempt a basic co-ordination of the arms and legs?

Intermediate

Lesson Plan 9 • 30 minutes

Themes and objectives: Reinforcing skills at the deep end

Introduction	**Theme of introduction** Your health and swimming.	**Introductory points/questions** Explanation of: • what swimming can do for the heart • how it can help with the breathing • how it helps to keep the body supple and flexible • how many people with different illnesses use the water for its benefits; give examples.
Skill/stroke practice	**Teaching progression** Working with the class in the deep end, revise some of the practices. Start with front crawl legs across the pool.	**Teaching tips** • Keep the chin close to the water's surface. • Look for a good flat body position and regular and consistent exhalation.
	Pupils experiment with front crawl in order to determine what suits them.	• Try shorter hand entry across widths and then try a longer hand entry. • Try different head positions when the head is centred at the front: first, look straight down at the bottom at 90 degrees; then straight in front under the surface at 180 degrees; finally, a mid position between the two. • Get pupils to explain how the different positions impact on their breathing.
	Pupils experiment with back crawl in order to determine what suits them.	• Try different hand entry positions: one with the outside of the upper arm very close to the ear, the other with the hands entering at about 2 o'clock and 10 o'clock from the head. • Swim widths working on different head positions: first, with the eyes fixed at 120 degrees right back on the ceiling; then with the chin tucked into the chest; finally, try the halfway point. • Ask pupils which was the most comfortable for them.
	Pupils work with single arm backstroke, first with the left arm and then with the right arm.	• The non-working arm should be placed in the water by the side of the body. • Pupils should be encouraged to concentrate on the little finger entering the water first. • Lift the shoulder as the arm is lifted from the water. It should produce a slight rolling action and the hand may go down further in the water when it is placed behind the head.
Contrasting activity	**Activity** Return to shallow water for a game of floating tag.	**Teaching tips** Pupils perform any different form of float to avoid being tagged. Pupils can only be tagged if they are not floating. The idea is to tag the whole class.
	Follow this with a game of porpoise tag.	The pupil who tags stands or treads water in the middle of the pool. Pupils swim across the width and duck underwater to avoid being tagged. They can only be tagged if they are on the surface or standing.
Evaluating lesson	**Main skill** The main purpose of the lesson has been to develop front crawl and back crawl skills in deep water.	**Points to watch out for** • Pupils should be able to swim comfortably with a good flat body position across the width of the pool. • They should be able to breathe easily without having to change the body position to take a breath.

Intermediate

Lesson Plan 10 • 30 minutes

Themes and objectives: Further skill reinforcing in deeper water

Introduction	**Theme of introduction** Explain what 'the catch' is in swimming and its importance.	**Introductory points/questions** • The catch' is the point where the hand starts to hold the water. • Analogy with rowing boat where the oar pulls to a certain point and the boat is pushed past the point where it starts to hold the water. • Ask pupils to describe where they think 'the catch' might be in their strokes.
Skill/stroke practice	**Teaching progression** The class works on breaststroke at the deep end of the pool.	**Teaching tips** • Work on pulling, kicking and gliding. • Try to think about where they might really 'catch' the water in breaststroke. • Work on a good whip with the ankles at the end of the kick.
	Experiment with different stroke rhythms.	• Try one arm pull and two or three kicks. • Pupils should try placing their face in the water with their eyes fixed immediately on the bottom during the recovery. • Then experiment with the eyes fixed in front in parallel with the surface of the water during the recovery phase. • Ask pupils which they find the most comfortable.
	The class moves on to experiment with the different feet-first entries.	• Try star and tuck shapes and entering with the hands above the head.
	Follow this with the head-first entries.	• Pupils should progress through the sitting, kneeling, crouching and standing dives. • Remember to follow earlier guidance on diving as diving needs to take place in a safe environment (*see* page 34).
	Pupils try the racing or plunge dive.	• Toes curled over the edge with the knees bent. • Hands can be positioned in front or behind the body. • Feet should be shoulder-width apart. • Pupils should look forward focusing on the point of entry. • Push with the feet and legs and bring the hands together so that the body is extended with the head between the arms. • Hands enter first followed by the rest of the body, as with other dives. • The entry and trajectory in the water is much flatter than with other dives.
Contrasting activity	**Activity** Shallow water activity: see-sawing with partner.	**Teaching tips** Pupils hold hands in pairs. One partner stands while the other sinks under the water as deep as possible. Then the position is reversed.
	Shallow water activity: alphabet float	Class members experiment with different floating positions, trying to form different letters of the alphabet.
Evaluating lesson	**Main skill** Building breaststroke and diving competences in deep water.	**Points to watch out for** • In breaststroke, can pupils swim in deep water with the right stroke timing? Do they breathe comfortably given the deep water? • In diving, do they find their way back to the surface easily? Do their fingers enter first with a nice, smooth arc?

Intermediate

Lesson Plan 11 • 30 minutes

Themes and objectives: Very basic introduction to life saving

Introduction	**Theme of introduction** The importance of being capable of saving lives.	**Introductory points/questions** • Explain that being able to save lives in water is often a matter of strength and knowledge. Knowledge is something that can be achieved now; strength is something that can be achieved when pupils are slightly older. • Explain why people get into difficulties, e.g. underestimate circumstances and overestimate own abilities.
Skill/stroke practice	**Teaching progression** Lifesaving stroke on back.	**Teaching tips** • The legs are similar to breaststroke but on the back. • The hands are lifted so as to be in line with the ears and then push back in a semi-circular motion to the hips. • At the same time, the lower legs bend at the knees to make the circular kicking motion. • The knees bend as the hands are lifted to the sides of the head. • Explain why this basic stroke is used in life saving.
	Pupils repeat the activity.	• Concentrate on tucking the chin to the chest to drop the knees under the water and create a more effective kick. • Pupils experiment with the head position until they can adopt the most effective position to get the best out of the leg kick. • Encourage pupils to look where they are going every three kicks.
	Life-saving side stroke: pupils experiment with the stroke on both sides.	• Pupils need to follow the pattern of breaststroke with their head permanently kept to one side. • One ear rests on the water. • The leading arm should stretch out well in front of the head at the start of the arm pull. • The trailing arm pulls under the water back towards the hips. • Pupils should try lying on the opposite side and should then determine which side they find easier to use.
	Ask the class to carry a series of objects from one side of the pool, keeping each object dry and landing it on the pool side opposite.	Explain the purpose is to give pupils the experience of swimming and working with their head high off the water.
Contrasting activity	**Activity** Fun swimming using one arm and one leg with as many variations as possible.	**Teaching tips** The most obvious examples are: • one-arm front crawl with and without the use of the legs • one-arm backstroke and dog paddle with and without the use of the legs • two-arm (simultaneous) backstroke with normal legs • one-arm breaststroke with and without legs. Ask pupils to note at which point in the stroke they can really feel that they are starting to grip on the water. Do they think this is the same point as when the normal full stroke is swum?
Evaluating lesson	**Main skill** Learning rudimentary life saving.	**Points to watch out for** • Have all pupils understood the relationship between the new strokes they have learnt and how they would be employed in a future life-saving situation? • Can they make elementary movements which follow the patterns of these strokes? • Can they hold their head clear of the water in a comfortable posture for all of the strokes practised?

Lesson Plan 12 • 30 minutes

Themes and objectives: Learning how to swim economically – getting the most out of each stroke swum

Introduction	**Theme of introduction** Explanation of buoyancy.	**Introductory points/questions** • Explain why some people sink more easily than others. • How you can prevent yourself from sinking. • How you can move and distribute your weight using different shapes in the water.
Skill/stroke practice	**Teaching progression** Working with front crawl, swim across the width counting the number of strokes it takes to get to the other side.	**Teaching tips** • First, pupils swim with their normal front crawl. • Ask them to really stretch and make each stroke more effective. Count the number of strokes again. • Now ask them to swim a third time and see if they can reduce the number of their strokes again. • Ask them how easy it would be to swim with this final version and whether they feel their swimming would benefit.
	Repeat the exercise with backstroke.	• Stress the importance of seeking the wall on backstroke and of attempting to reach for the wall with the fingers at long reach to reduce the number of strokes taken.
	Further repeat the exercise with breaststroke.	• Pupils should try a longer, wider pull and follow this with a smaller circle on the pull with a longer stretch forward on the recovery.
Contrasting activity	**Activity** Number retrieve.	**Teaching tips** • The class is split into a number of groups. • Pupils form a circle in the water and are given a number. • A sinking object is thrown into the middle of the circle and a number is called out. The relevant pupil has to retrieve the object.
Evaluating lesson	**Main skill** Improving the economy of each of the main three strokes.	**Points to watch out for** • Does reducing the number of strokes make pupils' swimming more efficient? • Do you feel it has a negative or positive effect on their stroke technique, body position and breathing? • Overall, how beneficial has it been to each pupil's individual strokes?

FURTHER INFORMATION RELATING TO SCHOOL SWIMMING

For general matters relating to swimming:
ASA Customer Services
Harold Fern House
Derby Square
Loughborough
Leicestershire
LE11 5AL
Tel: 0871 200 0928
E-mail: customerservices@swimming.org

For information on School Sport Partnerships:
Youth Sport Trust
Sir John Beckwith Centre for Sport
Loughborough University
Loughborough
Leicestershire
LE11 3TU
Tel: 01509 226600
E-mail: info@youthsporttrust.org

For information on school club links in relation to swimming:
ASA Customer Services
Harold Fern House
Derby Square
Loughborough
Leicestershire
LE11 5AL
Tel: 0871 200 0928
E-mail: customerservices@swimming.org

General information on the PE, School Sport and Club Links Strategy is available at the following web site: www.dfes.gov.uk/pess

Information on where to find qualified teachers:
Institute of Swimming
Harold Fern House
Derby Square
Loughborough
Leicestershire
LE11 5AL
Tel: 0871 200 0928
E-mail: ios@swimming.org.uk

British Swimming Coaches and Teachers Association
9 Kidderminster Road
Bromsgrove
Worcestershire
B61 7JJ
Tel: 0870 4288424
E-mail: enquiries@bscta.co.uk

For guidance on child protection:

- www.teachernet.gov.uk/management/childprotection

For guidance on minibus safety and other transport safety:

- www.rospa.com/roadsafety/advice/minibus/index.htm
- www.teachernet.gov.uk/management/healthandsafety

Where to find resources and equipment:

Institute of Sport and Recreation Management
Sir John Beckwith Centre for Sport
Loughborough University
Loughborough
Leicestershire
LE11 3TU
Tel: 01509 226474
E-mail: info@isrm.co.uk

ISRM has a complete range of video training packs, procedure manuals for pools and safety posters. Among other personnel, it is the body which represents swimming pool operators and management.

SwimGB
3 Decora Way
Luton
Bedfordshire
LU3 3HP
Tel: 01582 599252
E-mail: info@swimgb.co.uk

Swim GB keeps a complete range of ASA endorsed accessories and equipment for the pool side and the swimmer.

Information on finding suitable pools or for help in your own pool:

ASA Facilities Officer
Harold Fern House
Derby Square
Loughborough
Leicestershire
LE11 5AL
Tel: 0871 200 0928
E-mail: customerservices@swimming.org

Institute of Sport and Recreation Management
Sir John Beckwith Centre for Sport (address as above)

Information on water safety issues:

Royal Life Saving Society
River House
High Street
Broom
Warwickshire
B50 4HN
Tel: 01789 773994
E-mail: info@rlss.org.uk

Royal Society for the Prevention of Accidents
ROSPA House
Edgbaston Park
353 Bristol Road
Edgbaston
Birmingham
B5 7ST
Tel: 0121 248 2000
E-mail: help@rospa.com

Further information on water safety can be found on the Qualifications and Curriculum Authority swimming and water safety web site (www.nc.uk.net/safeswimming).

General issues on school swimming:
Department for Education and Skills swimming
PE & School Sports Team
3D, Sanctuary Buildings
Department for Education and Skills
Great Smith Street
London
SW1P 3BT
Tel: 0207 925 5950
E-mail: pe.sport@dfes.gsi.gov.uk

John Stiven, Esq.
General Secretary
English Schools Swimming Association
Mulina
Pyrford Woods
Pyrford
Woking
Surrey
GU22 8QT
01483 880650(o)
E-mail: j.stiven@essa-schoolswimming.com

Information on awards:
ASA Awards Centre
Unit 1
Kingfisher Enterprise Park
50 Arthur Street
Redditch
Worcestershire
B98 8LG
Tel (General Enquries): 01527 514288
Tel (Order No): 0800 220292
E-mail: salesawards@swimming.org

Swimming Teachers Association
Anchor House
Birch Street
Walsall
West Midlands
WS2 8HZ
Tel: 01922 645097
E-mail: sta@sta.co.uk

Information on Top Resources:

A series of 50 cards can be used by teachers to guide them through many of the early skills required by pupils when first starting to swim. These can be obtained from Youth Sport Trust at the Sir John Beckwith Centre for Sport (address as on page 94).

Printed literature:

The following is available from the ASA Awards Centre (address as on page 95):

- *Charter for Swimming for Schools*
- *Executive Summary of the Top-Up Pilot Schemes*
- *ASA National Curriculum Resource Pack*
- *ASA National Plan for Teaching Swimming*

The following titles are available from:
DfES Publications
P O Box 5050
Sherwood Park
Annesley
Nottinghamshire
NG15 0DJ
Tel: 0845 6022260
E-mail: dfes@prolog.uk.com

- *Learning through PE and Sport: A guide to the Physical Education, School Sport and Club Links Strategy* (reference LTPES2)
- *High quality PE and sport for young people: A guide to recognising and achieving high quality PE and sport in schools* (reference PE/HQ)

Schemes of work:

These are accessible from: www.standards.dfes.gov.uk/schemes.

Useful website addresses:

- Amateur Swimming Association – www.britishswimming.org
- Association for Physical Education – www.afpe.org.uk
- British Swimming Coaches and Teachers Association – www.bscta.com
- Department for Culture, Media and Sport – www.culture.gov.uk
- Department for Education and Skills – www.dfes.gov.uk
- English Schools Swimming Association – www.essa-schoolswimming.com
- Health and Safety Executive – www.hse.gov.uk
- Qualifications and Curriculum Authority Safe Swimming – www.nc.uk.net/safeswimming
- Royal Lifesaving Society – www.lifesavers.org.uk
- Royal Society for the Prevention of Accidents – www.rospa.co.uk
- Sports Coach UK – www.sportscoachuk.org
- Swimming Teachers Association – www.sta.co.uk